OUR SAVIOUR

The Work of Our Saviour
Past - Present - Future

by

Oliver B. Greene

The Gospel Hour, Inc.
Oliver B. Greene, Director
Box 2024, Greenville, South Carolina 29602

First printing, April 1969—15,000 copies
Second printing, July 1969—15,000 copies
Third printing, September 1971—15,000 copies

$5.00

FOREWORD

There is much confusion among Christians—ministers and laymen alike—concerning the past, present, and future work of our Saviour, the Lord Jesus Christ. Many people are not able to rightly divide the Word of Truth in relation to His *past* work as our Redeemer, His *present* work as our Saviour and High Priest, and His *future* work as King of kings and Lord of lords.

Christ's work of redemption is threefold, and it is by virtue of His threefold work that believers are saved from the *penalty* of sin (past), saved daily from the *power* of sin (present), and *will be* saved from the very *presence* of sin (future).

There is also much confusion and misunderstanding concerning the *resurrections* (plural) and the *judgments* (also plural). It is the aim and hope of the author to clarify at least some of these points, thus helping Christians to reach new depths of understanding of the believer's position in this present world, and at the same time helping the unsaved to catch a clearer vision of the joy and glories of salvation.

May God use these pages to His glory.

—Oliver B. Greene

CONTENTS

OUR SAVIOUR

The Work of Our Saviour, the Lord Jesus Christ
Past—Present—Future

OUR SAVIOUR

His Work—Past, Present, and Future

Introduction

The Word of God clearly reveals that all things were created by and for the Lord Jesus Christ, the Son of God, "who is *the image* of the invisible God, the firstborn of every creature: for by Him were all things created, that are in heaven, and that are in earth, visible and invisible, whether they be thrones, or dominions, or principalities, or powers: all things were created by Him, and for Him: and He is before all things, and by Him all things consist" (Col. 1:15—17).

God is perfect. Therefore when He created this universe and everything in it His creation was perfect. But when Adam fell, God's perfect creation was marred and scarred by the entrance of sin, it was brought into bondage and corruption, and the work of redemption became a necessity. Since no creature of God was capable of or fitted for the work of redeeming lost man and delivering the whole creation from corruption, the only One who could bring about redemption was the Son of God, the Creator Himself—yea, very God in flesh. He alone could undertake and perform the mighty work of redemption. All things are to the honor and glory of God, but to accomplish this, God had to appear on this earth in the form of man—and

9

He did exactly that:

"All things are of God, who hath reconciled us to Himself by Jesus Christ, and hath given to us the ministry of reconciliation; to wit, that God was in Christ, reconciling the world unto Himself, not imputing their trespasses unto them; and hath committed unto us the word of reconciliation" (II Cor. 5:18,19).

"There is therefore now no condemnation to them which are in Christ Jesus, who walk not after the flesh, but after the Spirit. For the law of the Spirit of life in Christ Jesus hath made me free from the law of sin and death. For what the law could not do, in that it was weak through the flesh, God sending His own Son in the likeness of sinful flesh, and for sin, condemned sin in the flesh: that the righteousness of the law might be fulfilled in us, who walk not after the flesh, but after the Spirit" (Rom. 8:1—4).

The work of Christ is threefold—past, present, and future—and it will terminate when He delivers up the kingdom to God the Father, that God may be all in all:

"Then cometh the end, when He shall have delivered up the kingdom to God, even the Father; when He shall have put down all rule and all authority and power. For He must reign, till He hath put all enemies under His feet. The last enemy that shall be destroyed is death. For He hath put all things under His feet. But when He saith all things are put under Him, it is manifest that He is excepted, which did put all things under Him. And when all things shall be subdued unto Him, then shall the Son also Himself be subject unto Him that put all things under Him, that God may be all in all" (I Cor. 15:24—28).

This threefold aspect of the work of Christ corresponds to His threefold office of Prophet, Priest, and

King, as set forth in the Word of God.

The redemptive work of Christ has a very special meaning for the Church. In Paul's letter to the Ephesian believers we read, "Husbands, love your wives, even as Christ also loved the Church, and gave Himself for it; that He might sanctify and cleanse it with the washing of water by the Word, that He might present it to Himself a glorious Church, not having spot, or wrinkle, or any such thing; but that it should be holy and without blemish" (Eph. 5:25—27). We see Christ's threefold work here, in that He loved the Church and gave Himself for it—work that has been accomplished and is therefore past. Since then, He sanctifies the Church by the washing of water by the Word—present tense. In the future, He will present the Church to Himself, a glorious Church without spot or wrinkle.

By virtue of Christ's threefold work, believers are saved from the *penalty* of sin (past), we *are* being saved from the *power* of sin (present), and we *will be* saved from the very *presence* of sin (future).

His threefold work also has significance for the people of Israel. He came as their Messiah, He died on the cross for their sins. During this present age God's earthly people are not forgotten or cast away. They are miraculously preserved, they continue to be a separated people. And in the future—no one knows the day—He will return for the Church, and in the second phase of His second coming He will return to Israel as their Redeemer to claim them as His purchased possession. He will then bring them into their right relationship to Himself.

Many Christians are ignorant of what the finished work of Christ actually means to us, and because of this ignorance they are forever trying to do what the

Lord God Almighty has *already done for them.* Still others are ignorant concerning the believer's position in Christ even at this very moment, and they know next to nothing about the priestly work of the Saviour as He is now seated at the right hand of God, making intercession for His own. Confusion concerning the future work of Christ as King is alarming the great majority of Christians today. Very few distinguish between the Jew, the Gentile, and the Church of God. They take the promises of the Kingdom and give them to the Church, and this is spiritual robbery.

In this study we will allow the Holy Spirit to enlighten us and lead us into deeper truths concerning the past, present, and future work of our wonderful Lord and Saviour, Jesus Christ, and as we study to rightly divide the Word of Truth, the following passages will be of great help to us:

"These words spake Jesus, and lifted up His eyes to heaven, and said, Father, the hour is come; glorify thy Son, that thy Son also may glorify thee: As thou hast given Him power over all flesh, that He should give eternal life to as many as thou hast given Him. And this is life eternal, that they might know thee the only true God, and Jesus Christ, whom thou hast sent.

"I have glorified thee on the earth: I have finished the work which thou gavest me to do. And now, O Father, glorify thou me with thine own self with the glory which I had with thee before the world was. I have manifested thy name unto the men which thou gavest me out of the world: thine they were, and thou gavest them me; and they have kept thy word. Now they have known that all things whatsoever thou hast given me are of thee. For I have given unto them the words which thou gavest me; and they have received them, and have known surely that I came out from thee, and they have believed that thou didst send me.

"I pray for them: I pray not for the world, but for them which thou hast given me; for they are thine. And all mine are thine, and thine are mine; and I am glorified in them. And now I am no more in the world, but these are in the world, and I come to thee. Holy Father, keep through thine own name those whom thou hast given me, that they may be one, as we are. While I was with them in the world, I kept them in thy name: those that thou gavest me I have kept, and none of them is lost, but the son of perdition; that the Scripture might be fulfilled.

"And now come I to thee; and these things I speak in the world, that they might have my joy fulfilled in themselves. I have given them thy Word; and the world hath hated them, because they are not of the world, even as I am not of the world. I pray not that thou shouldest take them out of the world, but that thou shouldest keep them from the evil. They are not of the world, even as I am not of the world.

"Sanctify them through thy truth: thy Word is truth. As thou hast sent me into the world, even so have I also sent them into the world. And for their sakes I sanctify myself, that they also might be sanctified through the truth. Neither pray I for these alone, but for them also which shall believe on me through their word; that they all may be one; as thou, Father, art in me, and I in thee, that they also may be one in us: that the world may believe that thou hast sent me. And the glory which thou gavest me I have given them; that they may be one, even as we are one: I in them, and thou in me, that they may be made perfect in one; and that the world may know that thou hast sent me, and hast loved them, as thou hast loved me.

"Father, I will that they also, whom thou hast given me, be with me where I am; that they may behold my glory, which thou hast given me: for thou lovedst me before the foundation of the world. O righteous Father, the world hath not known

13

thee: but I have known thee, and these have known that
thou hast sent me. And I have declared unto them thy name,
and will declare it: that the love wherewith thou hast loved
me may be in them, and I in them" (John 17:1—26).

5:10

"For the law having a shadow of good things to come, and
not the very image of the things, can never with those sacrifices which they offered year by year continually make the
comers thereunto perfect. For then would they not have ceased
to be offered? because that the worshippers once purged should
have had no more conscience of sins. But in those sacrifices
there is a remembrance again made of sins every year. For
it is not possible that the blood of bulls and of goats should
take away sins.

"Wherefore when He cometh into the world, He said, Sacrifice and offering thou wouldest not, but a body hast thou prepared me: In burnt-offerings and sacrifices for sin thou hast
had no pleasure. Then said I, Lo, I come (in the volume of
the book it is written of me,) to do thy will, O God. Above
when He said, Sacrifice and offering and burnt-offerings and
offering for sin thou wouldest not, neither hadst pleasure therein; which are offered by the law. Then said He, Lo, I come
to do thy will, O God. He taketh away the first, that He
may establish the second. By the which will we are sanctified
through the offering of the body of Jesus Christ once for all.

"And every priest standeth daily ministering and offering
oftentimes the same sacrifices, which can never take away
sins: but this Man, after He had offered one sacrifice for
sins for ever, sat down on the right hand of God; from henceforth expecting till His enemies be made His footstool. For
by one offering He hath perfected for ever them that are
sanctified. Whereof the Holy Ghost also is a witness to us:
for after that He had said before, This is the covenant that
I will make with them after those days, saith the Lord, I
will put my laws into their hearts, and in their minds will

I write them; and their sins and iniquities will I remember no more. Now where remission of these is, there is no more offering for sin.

"Having therefore, brethren, boldness to enter into the holiest by the blood of Jesus, by a new and living way, which He hath consecrated for us, through the veil, that is to say, His flesh; and having an high priest over the house of God; let us draw near with a true heart in full assurance of faith, having our hearts sprinkled from an evil conscience, and our bodies washed with pure water. Let us hold fast the profession of our faith without wavering; (for He is faithful that promised;) and let us consider one another to provoke unto love and to good works: not forsaking the assembling of ourselves together, as the manner of some is; but exhorting one another: and so much the more, as ye see the day approaching" (Heb. 10:1—25).

Chapter I

THE PAST WORK OF CHRIST

"I have greater witness than that of John: for the works which the Father hath given me to finish, the same works that I do, bear witness of me, that the Father hath sent me" (John 5:36).

"I must work the works of Him that sent me, while it is day: the night cometh, when no man can work" (John 9:4).

"Believest thou not that I am in the Father, and the Father in me? The words that I speak unto you I speak not of myself: but the Father that dwelleth in me, He doeth the works" (John 14:10).

Throughout the Old Testament Scriptures we see the work of the Lord Jesus Christ foreshadowed and prophesied in various ways. From time to time a Supernatural Being appeared on earth, and that Supernatural Being was none other than God's Son, the Lord Jesus Christ. As soon as sin entered the Garden of Eden, He appeared on the scene seeking and calling for Adam and Eve.

Satan entered the garden where God had placed the man and woman. He entered in the form of a serpent, a subtle creature, and approached Eve with a question: *"Hath God said,* Ye shall not eat of every tree of the garden?"* Eve gave audience to the devil, and replied, "We may eat of the fruit of the trees of the garden: but of the fruit of the tree which is in the midst of the garden, God hath said, *Ye shall not eat of it, neither shall ye TOUCH it, LEST ye die.*" God had commanded Adam and Eve not to *eat* of the tree of the knowledge of good and evil, but He had said nothing about *touching* it, so Eve added to what God said. She also *softened* what He said—i. e., God warned, "Thou shalt *SURELY die,*" and Eve quoted Him as saying, *"Lest* ye die."

The serpent knew what God had said, and when he realized that Eve had misquoted God he then very subtly branded the Almighty a liar: *"Thou shalt NOT surely die!"* Then he suggested to Eve that God was unfair, that He knew if she and her husband ate of the fruit of that particular tree their eyes would be opened and they would be as gods, knowing good and evil.

So Eve *looked* at the tree, she saw that it was pleasant to look upon, it was good for food, and she wanted to be wise. Therefore she took of the fruit, she ate, she gave to Adam and he ate. Immediately "the eyes of them both were opened, and they knew that they were naked." Shocked by the shamefulness of their discovery, they sewed fig leaves together and made aprons with which they attempted to cover their nakedness—but they could not hide the shame of their guilty hearts.

Manifestations of Jehovah in the Old Testament Scriptures

To Adam:—
Now we come to the first appearance on earth of the Supernatural Being from heaven, seeking the lost: "They heard the voice of the Lord God walking in

the garden in the cool of the day: and Adam and his wife hid themselves from the presence of the Lord God amongst the trees of the garden. *And the Lord God called unto Adam, and said unto him, WHERE ART THOU?"* (Gen. 3:8, 9).

In John 1:1, 2, 14 we read, *"In the beginning was the Word,* and the Word was *with* God, and *the Word WAS God.* The same was in the beginning with God. ... And *the Word was made flesh,* and dwelt among us, (and we beheld His glory, the glory as of the only begotten of the Father,) full of grace and truth." So the One who walked in the garden was the Word of God, yes, none other than the Christ. Jesus of Nazareth was born of the Virgin Mary some two thousand years ago; *but God's CHRIST was in the beginning.* "The Word" was in the beginning, and it was the Word, the Christ of God, who walked in the garden calling, "Adam, where art thou?"

Adam and Eve made excuses for what they had done. Adam explained, "I heard thy voice ... I was afraid because I was naked ... I hid myself." God then asked, "Who *told* thee that thou wast naked? Hast thou eaten of the tree, whereof I commanded thee that thou shouldest not eat?" Then Adam offered another excuse—he blamed Eve: *"The woman whom thou gavest to be with me,* she gave me of the tree, and I did eat." Eve of course blamed the serpent. She said, *"The serpent beguiled me,* and I did eat."

God then said to the serpent, "Because thou hast done this, thou art cursed above all cattle, and above every beast of the field. Upon thy belly shalt thou go, and dust shalt thou eat all the days of thy life! *And I will put enmity between thee and the woman, and between thy seed and her seed; IT SHALL BRUISE THY HEAD, AND THOU SHALT BRUISE*

19

HIS HEEL." (Please read Genesis 3:1—15.)

Here in verse 15 we see the first prophecy having to do with the coming of the Eternal Word in flesh—a prophecy fulfilled "in the fulness of the time" as recorded in Galatians 4:4,5 when "God sent forth His Son, made of a woman, made under the law, to redeem them that were under the law, that we might receive the adoption of sons."

In Genesis 3:15 God clearly indicated the incarnation of Christ, His redemptive work on the cross, and His final victory over Satan. The coats of skins with which God clothed Adam and Eve, at the expense of the blood of innocent animals (Gen. 3:21), typified the atoning sacrifice of the Lord Jesus Christ when His blood should be shed for the redemption of sinners.

To Abraham:—

In the eighteenth chapter of Genesis we read:

"The Lord appeared unto (Abraham) in the plains of Mamre: and he sat in the tent door in the heat of the day; and he lift up his eyes and looked, and, lo, three men stood by him: and when he saw them, he ran to meet them from the tent door, and bowed himself toward the ground, and said: *MY LORD, if now I have found favour in thy sight, pass not away, I pray thee, from thy servant:* Let a little water, I pray you, be fetched, and wash your feet, and rest yourselves under the tree: and I will fetch a morsel of bread, and comfort ye your hearts; after that ye shall pass on: for therefore are ye come to your servant. And they said, So do, as thou hast said.

"And Abraham hastened into the tent unto Sarah, and said, Make ready quickly three measures of fine meal, knead it, and make cakes upon the hearth. And Abraham ran unto the herd, and fetcht a calf tender and good, and gave it unto a young man; and he hasted to dress it. And he took butter, and milk, and the calf which he had dressed, and set it before them; and he stood by them under the tree, and they did eat. And they said unto him, Where is Sarah thy wife? And he said, Behold, in the tent. And He said, I will certainly return unto thee according to the time of life, and, lo, Sarah thy wife shall have a son. And Sarah heard it in the tent door, which was behind Him.

"Now Abraham and Sarah were old and well stricken in age; and it ceased to be with Sarah after the manner of women. Therefore Sarah laughed within herself, saying, After I am waxed old shall I have pleasure, my lord being old also? And *the Lord* said unto Abraham, Wherefore did Sarah laugh, saying, Shall I of a surety bear a child, which am old? *Is any thing too hard for the Lord?* At the time appointed I will return unto thee, according to the time of life, and Sarah shall have a son.

"Then Sarah denied, saying, I laughed not; for she was afraid. And He said, Nay; but thou didst laugh. And the men rose up from thence, and looked toward Sodom: and Abraham went with them to bring them on the way. *And the Lord said,* Shall I hide from Abraham that thing which I do; seeing that Abraham shall surely become a great and mighty nation, and all the nations of the earth shall be blessed in him? For I know him, that he will command his children and his household after him, and they shall keep the way of the Lord, to do justice and judgment; that the Lord may bring upon Abraham that which He hath spoken of him.

"*And the Lord said,* Because the cry of Sodom and Gomorrah is great, and because their sin is very grievous; I will go down now, and see whether they have done altogether according to the cry of it, which is come unto me; and if not, I will know.

"*And the men turned their faces from thence, and went toward Sodom: BUT ABRAHAM STOOD YET BEFORE THE LORD*" (Gen. 18:1–22).

21

In this passage, Jehovah appeared in visible form. He came to faithful Abraham as a traveler. He was accompanied by two angels, He ate in Abraham's presence, *Abraham addressed Him as "LORD," and worshipped Him.*

In the remaining verses in that chapter we find the account of Abraham's pleading with the Lord on behalf of the wicked cities of Sodom and Gomorrah, his fruitless search for even *ten* righteous men in those cities, and then in verse 33 we read: *"And the LORD went His way, as soon as He had left communing with Abraham:* and Abraham returned unto his place."

To Jacob:—

"And Jacob was left alone; and there wrestled a Man with him until the breaking of the day. And when He saw that He prevailed not against him, He touched the hollow of his thigh; and the hollow of Jacob's thigh was out of joint, as he wrestled with Him.

"And He said, Let me go, for the day breaketh. And he said, I will not let thee go, except thou bless me. And He said unto him, What is thy name? And he said, Jacob. And He said, Thy name shall be called no more Jacob, but Israel: for as a prince hast thou power with God and with men, and hast prevailed. And Jacob asked Him, and said, Tell me, I pray thee, thy name. And He said, Wherefore is it that thou dost ask after my name? And He blessed him there.

"And Jacob called the name of the place Peniel: for *I have seen GOD face to face, and my life is preserved.* And as he passed over Penuel the sun rose upon him, and he halted upon his thigh. Therefore

22

the children of Israel eat not of the sinew which shrank, which is upon the hollow of the thigh, unto this day: because He touched the hollow of Jacob's thigh in the sinew that shrank" (Gen. 32:24—32).

The Man who wrestled with Jacob at Peniel was none other than the Lord Jesus Christ. Later Jacob referred to Him as "the Angel which redeemed me" (Gen. 48:16). Repeatedly we read of Him as "the Angel of the Lord"—not a created angel, but an uncreated Being.

To Moses:—

"Now Moses kept the flock of Jethro his father in law, the priest of Midian: and he led the flock to the backside of the desert, and came to the mountain of God, even to Horeb. And the Angel of the Lord appeared unto him in a flame of fire out of the midst of a bush: and he looked, and, behold, the bush burned with fire, and the bush was not consumed. And Moses said, I will now turn aside, and see this great sight, why the bush is not burnt.

"And when the Lord saw that he turned aside to see, *God called unto him out of the midst of the bush, and said, Moses, Moses.* And he said, Here am I. And He said, Draw not nigh hither: put off thy shoes from off thy feet, for the place whereon thou standest is holy ground. Moreover He said, *I am the God of thy father, the God of Abraham, the God of Isaac, and the God of Jacob. And Moses hid his face; for he was afraid to look upon God.*

"And the Lord said, I have surely seen the affliction of my people which are in Egypt, and have heard their cry by reason of their taskmasters; for I know their sorrows; and I am come down to deliver them out of the hand of the Egyptians, and to bring them up out of that land unto a good land and a large, unto a land flowing with milk and honey; unto the place of the Canaanites, and the Hittites, and the

Amorites, and the Perizzites, and the Hivites, and the Jebusites.

"Now therefore, behold, the cry of the children of Israel is come unto me: and I have also seen the oppression wherewith the Egyptians oppress them. Come now therefore, and I will send thee unto Pharaoh, that thou mayest bring forth my people the children of Israel out of Egypt.

"And Moses said unto God, Who am I, that I should go unto Pharaoh, and that I should bring forth the children of Israel out of Egypt? And He said, Certainly I will be with thee; and this shall be a token unto thee, that I have sent thee: When thou hast brought forth the people out of Egypt, ye shall serve God upon this mountain.

"And Moses said unto God, Behold, when I come unto the children of Israel, and shall say unto them, The God of your fathers hath sent me unto you; and they shall say to me, What is His name? what shall I say unto them? *And God said unto Moses, I AM THAT I AM:* and He said, *Thus shalt thou say unto the children of Israel, I AM HATH SENT ME UNTO YOU"* (Ex. 3:1—14).

Moses stood in the presence of Almighty God as He spoke to him from the burning bush, and although He is spoken of as "the Angel of the Lord" (v. 2), He revealed Himself as Jehovah God and made His name known unto Moses.

To Joshua:—

"And it came to pass, when Joshua was by Jericho, that he lifted up his eyes and looked, and, behold, there stood a Man over against him with His sword drawn in His hand: and Joshua went unto Him, and said unto Him, Art thou for us, or for our adversaries? And He said, Nay; but as *Captain of the host of the Lord* am I now come. And Joshua fell on his face to the earth, and did worship, and said unto Him,

24

What saith my Lord unto His servant? And *the Captain of the Lord's host* said unto Joshua, Loose thy shoe from off thy foot; for the place whereon thou standest is holy. And Joshua did so" (Josh. 5:13—15).

The "Captain of the Lord's host" was none other than the Lord God Almighty.

To Israel:—

"The Lord went before them by day in a pillar of a cloud, to lead them the way; and by night in a pillar of fire, to give them light; to go by day and night: He took not away the pillar of the cloud by day, nor the pillar of fire by night, from before the people" (Ex. 13:21, 22).

Jehovah God was with His elect nation in the wilderness. He dwelt with them in the glory cloud. He guided them, supplied their every need. He protected them, judged them, and overthrew their enemies.

To Manoah:—

"And the Angel of the Lord said unto Manoah, Though thou detain me, I will not eat of thy bread: and if thou wilt offer a burnt-offering, thou must offer it unto the Lord. For Manoah knew not that He was an Angel of the Lord. And Manoah said unto the Angel of the Lord, What is thy name, that when thy sayings come to pass we may do thee honour?

"And the Angel of the Lord said unto him, Why askest thou thus after my name, seeing it is secret? So Manoah took a kid with a meat-offering, and offered it upon a rock unto the Lord: and the Angel did wonderously; and Manoah and his wife looked on. For it came to pass, when the flame went up toward heaven from off the altar, that the Angel of the Lord ascended in the flame of the altar. And Manoah and his wife looked on it, and fell on their faces to the ground.

"But the Angel of the Lord did no more appear to Manoah and to his wife. Then Manoah knew that He was an Angel of the Lord. And Manoah said unto his wife, *We shall surely die, because WE HAVE SEEN GOD.* But his wife said unto him, If the Lord were pleased to kill us, He would not have received a burnt-offering and a meat-offering at our hands, neither would He have shewed us all these things, nor would as at this time have told us such things as these" (Judges 13:16—23).

This man of God and his wife saw Jehovah ascend in the smoke and fire of sacrifice.

To Isaiah:—

"In the year that King Uzziah died I saw also the Lord sitting upon a throne, high and lifted up, and His train filled the temple. Above it stood the seraphims: each one had six wings; with twain he covered his face, and with twain he covered his feet, and with twain he did fly. And one cried unto another, and said, Holy, holy, holy, is the Lord of hosts: the whole earth is full of His glory. And the posts of the door moved at the voice of him that cried, and the house was filled with smoke. Then said I, Woe is me! for I am undone; because I am a man of unclean lips, and I dwell in the midst of a people of unclean lips: *for mine eyes have seen the King, THE LORD OF HOSTS"* (Isa. 6:1—5).

Thus did Isaiah gaze upon God's glory and realize his own unworthiness. But after being cleansed he was given God's message to Israel, His warning and His prophecy of the fulfillment of His promise of Genesis 3:15.

To Ezekiel:—

"And I looked, and, behold, a whirlwind came out of the north, a great cloud, and a fire infolding itself, and a brightness was about it, and out of the midst thereof as the colour of amber, out of the midst of the fire. Also out of the midst thereof came the likeness of four living creatures. And this was their appearance; they had the likeness of a man. And every one had four faces, and every one had four wings. . . . And there was a voice from the firmament that was over their heads, when they stood, and had let down their wings. And above the firmament that was over their heads was the likeness of a throne, as the appearance of a sapphire stone: and upon the likeness of the throne was the likeness as the appearance of a Man above upon it. And I saw as the colour of amber, as the appearance of fire round about within it, from the appearance of His loins even upward, and from the appearance of His loins even downward, I saw as it were the appearance of fire, and it had brightness round about. As the appearance of the bow that is in the cloud in the day of rain, so was the appearance of the bright-ness round about. *This was the appearance of the likeness of the glory of the LORD. And when I saw it, I FELL UPON MY FACE, and I heard a voice of One that spake*" (Ezek. 1:4—6, 25—28).

Afterward, Ezekiel was filled with the Spirit and commissioned of God to carry His message to Israel.

To Nebuchadnezzar:—

"And he (Nebuchadnezzar) commanded the most mighty men that were in his army to bind Shadrach, Meshach, and Abednego, and to cast them into the burning fiery furnace. Then these men were bound in their coats, their hosen, and their hats, and their other garments, and were cast into the midst of the burning fiery furnace. Therefore because the king's commandment was urgent, and the furnace exceeding hot, the flame of the fire slew those men that took up Shadrach, Meshach, and Abednego. And these three men, Shadrach, Meshach, and Abednego, fell down bound into the midst of the burning fiery furnace.

"Then Nebuchadnezzar the king was astonied, and rose up in haste, and spake, and said unto his counsellors, Did not we cast *three* men bound into the midst of the fire? They answered and said unto the king, True, O king. He answered and said, *Lo, I see four men loose, walking in the midst of the fire, and they have no hurt; and THE FORM OF THE FOURTH IS LIKE THE SON OF GOD"* (Dan. 3: 20–25).

This king had spent his life in building a world empire to satisfy his own ego and pride; but if you will follow his history as recorded in chapters 3 and 4 of the book of Daniel you will see that following this incident at the fiery furnace he was converted and proclaimed the supremacy of Jehovah God throughout the land.

To Daniel: —

"In the third year of Cyrus king of Persia a thing was revealed unto Daniel, whose name was called Belteshazzar; and the thing was true, but the time appointed was long: and he understood the thing, and had understanding of the vision. In those days I Daniel was mourning three full weeks. I ate no pleasant bread, neither came flesh nor wine in my mouth, neither did I anoint myself at all, till three whole

28

weeks were fulfilled. And in the four and twentieth day of the first month, as I was by the side of the great river, which is Hiddekel, then I lifted up mine eyes, and looked, and behold a certain Man clothed in linen, whose loins were girded with fine gold of Uphaz: His body also was like the beryl, and His face as the appearance of lightning, and His eyes as lamps of fire, and His arms and His feet like in colour to polished brass, and the voice of His words like the voice of a multitude. And I Daniel alone saw the vision: for the men that were with me saw not the vision; but a great quaking fell upon them, so that they fled to hide themselves. Therefore I was left alone, and saw this great vision, and there remained no strength in me: for my comeliness was turned in me into corruption, and *I retained no strength. Yet heard I the voice of His words: and when I heard the voice of His words, then was I in a deep sleep on my face, and my face toward the ground"* (Dan. 10:1−9).

Daniel describes the same Person seen and described by John the Beloved in Revelation 1:9−18 − the Son of God.

All of these passages foreshadow the two great manifestations of the Lord Jesus Christ here on earth, and both manifestations are necessary to His work. He came the first time in humiliation, as a Lamb to be led to the slaughter. He will come the second time as the Lion of the Tribe of Judah, in power and great glory.

The Person who appeared in the form of the Word in the Garden of Eden, the Person who appeared to Abraham, Isaac, Jacob, and the other Old Testament saints, is the same Person who appeared to the two disciples on the road to Emmaus and to the disciples in the upper room, as recorded in Luke 24:13—45.

Other Foreshadowings
of the Work of the Lord Jesus Christ

In the Old Testament Scriptures, all of the divinely-given institutions (and many of the historical events) foreshadow the work of the Lamb of God, the Lord Jesus Christ. History, as recorded in the Old Testament, is the preliminary history of His Incarnation. The whole sacrificial system of the Levitical priesthood foretold His great redemptive work. Each offering and sacrifice revealed the different phases of His work on the cross, as well as His holy and spotless humanity.

The sufferings of the Lamb of God and their meaning for lost sinners were thus made known in the Old Testament. In Genesis chapter 4 we find recorded the first blood-offering *by man*. God shed the blood of innocent animals to provide covering for Adam and Eve, but *Abel brought a lamb* and in faith offered it unto the Lord. Hebrews 11:4 tells us, *"By faith* Abel offered unto God a more excellent sacrifice than Cain, by which he obtained witness that he was righteous, God testifying of his gifts: *and by it he being dead yet speaketh."*

From Abel's lamb to the last lamb to die before the sacrifice of the true Lamb of God with His victorious cry *"It is finished!"* the innumerable thousands of turtle doves, lambs, bulls, and goats slain in sacrifice were types of *the one sacrifice* offered on Calvary's rugged cross. The Lamb of God answered all of the events and institutions of the sacrificial system of offerings. The holy days and holidays, the feasts and festivals, were finished when the Lord Jesus Christ finished His work on earth and declared it so. Further-

30

more, if the Son of God had *not* died on the cross, all of the *symbolic* offerings would have been in vain because *they all pointed to Calvary!*

The Tabernacle is often mentioned in the Old Testament economy, and all of its appointments down to the very least detail had some meaning relating to the Person of the Lord Jesus Christ who finished the wonderful work of redemption: "For unto us a Child is born, unto us a Son is given: and the government shall be upon His shoulder: and His name shall be called Wonderful, Counsellor, The mighty God, The everlasting Father, The Prince of Peace. Of the increase of His government and peace there shall be no end, upon the throne of David, and upon His kingdom, to order it, and to establish it with judgment and with justice from henceforth even for ever. The zeal of the Lord of hosts will perform this" (Isa. 9:6, 7).

The Passover presents a perfect picture of Calvary—the Lamb of God, His shed blood, and deliverance through the blood:

"The Lord spake unto Moses and Aaron in the land of Egypt, saying, This month shall be unto you the beginning of months: it shall be the first month of the year to you. Speak ye unto all the congregation of Israel, saying, In the tenth day of this month they shall take to them every man a lamb, according to the house of their fathers, a lamb for an house: and if the household be too little for the lamb, let him and his neighbour next unto his house take it according to the number of the souls; every man according to his eating shall make your count for the lamb.

"Your lamb shall be without blemish, a male of the first year: ye shall take it out from the sheep, or from the goats: and ye shall keep it up until the fourteenth day of the same month: and the whole assembly of the congregation of Israel shall kill it in the evening. And they shall take of the blood, and strike it on the two side posts and on the upper door post of the houses, wherein they shall eat it. And they shall eat the flesh in that night, roast with fire, and unleavened bread; and with bitter herbs they shall eat it. Eat not of it raw, nor sodden at all with water, but roast with fire; his head with his legs, and with the purtenance thereof.

"And ye shall let nothing of it remain until the morning; and that which remaineth of it until the morning ye shall burn with fire. And thus shall ye eat it; with your loins girded, your shoes on your feet, and your staff in your hand; and ye shall eat it in haste: it is the Lord's Passover. For I will pass through the land of Egypt this night, and will smite all the firstborn in the land of Egypt, both man and beast; and against all the gods of Egypt I will execute judgment: I am the Lord. *And the blood shall be to you for a token upon the houses where ye are: and WHEN I SEE THE BLOOD, I WILL PASS OVER YOU,* and the plague shall not be upon you to destroy you, when I smite the land of Egypt" (Ex. 12:1–13).

The brazen serpent lifted up by Moses in the wilderness also points to Calvary:

"The people spake against God, and against Moses, Wherefore have ye brought us up out of Egypt to die in the wilderness? for there is no bread, neither is there any water; and our soul loatheth this light bread. And the Lord sent fiery serpents among the people, and they bit the people; and much people of Israel died. Therefore the people came to Moses, and said, We have sinned, for we have spoken against the Lord, and against thee. Pray unto the Lord, that He take away the serpents from us. And Moses prayed for the people.

"And the Lord said unto Moses, *Make thee a fiery serpent, and set it upon a pole: and it shall come to pass, that every one that is bitten, when he looketh*

32

upon it, shall live. And Moses made a serpent of brass, and put it upon a pole, and it came to pass, that if a serpent had bitten any man, when he beheld the serpent of brass, he lived" (Num. 21:5—9).

Jesus referred back to this serpent of brass in His conversation with Nicodemus. In John 3:14, 15 we read, *"And as Moses lifted up the serpent in the wilderness, EVEN SO must the Son of man be lifted up: that whosoever believeth in Him should not perish, but have eternal life."* Thus the Lord Jesus Christ pointed to the serpent of brass, lifted up in the wilderness, as a perfect picture of Himself lifted up on Calvary's cross.

The offering of Isaac presents a magnificent picture of God the Father giving His only begotten Son to die that you and I might be saved:

"And it came to pass after these things, that God did tempt Abraham, and said unto him, Abraham: and he said, Behold, here I am. And He said, *Take now thy son, thine only son Isaac, whom thou lovest, and get thee into the land of Moriah; and offer him there for a burnt-offering upon one of the mountains which I will tell thee of.*

"And Abraham rose up early in the morning, and saddled his ass, and took two of his young men with him, and Isaac his son, and clave the wood for the burnt-offering, and rose up, and went unto the place of which God had told him. Then on the third day Abraham lifted up his eyes, and saw the place afar off.

"And Abraham said unto his young men, Abide ye here with the ass; and I and the lad will go yonder and worship, and come again to you. And Abraham took the wood of the burnt-offering, and laid it upon Isaac his son; and he took the fire in his hand, and a knife; and they went both of them together. And Isaac spake unto Abraham his father, and said, My father: and he said, Here am I, my son. And he said,

33

Behold the fire and the wood: *but where is the lamb for a burnt-offering?* And Abraham said, *My son, God will provide Himself a lamb for a burnt-offering.* So they went both of them together.

"And they came to the place which God had told him of; and Abraham built an altar there, and laid the wood in order, and bound Isaac his son, and laid him on the altar upon the wood. And Abraham stretched forth his hand, and took the knife to slay his son. And the angel of the Lord called unto him out of heaven, and said, Abraham, Abraham: and he said, Here am I. And he said, Lay not thine hand upon the lad, neither do thou any thing unto him: for now I know that thou fearest God, seeing thou hast not withheld thy son, thine only son from me. *And Abraham lifted up his eyes, and looked, and behold behind him a ram caught in a thicket by his horns: and Abraham went and took the ram, and offered him up for a burnt-offering IN THE STEAD OF HIS SON*" (Gen. 22:1—13).

The words in verse 7 seem to indicate that Isaac had a premonition that he himself was to be the lamb. This was true of the Lamb of God. When He left the Father's bosom and all the glories of heaven, He knew that He was coming into a world that would reject Him, and that He would offer Himself as a sacrifice on Mount Calvary—the *one and only* sacrifice that could pay sin's debt and satisfy the holiness of God. And whereas God *spared Isaac* and provided a ram in his place, *He could not spare HIS OWN SON.* It was a divine imperative that Jesus, the Lamb of God without blemish and without spot, be lifted up on the cross and shed His blood for the sin of the world.

Direct Prophecies
Concerning Christ's Coming and His Work

"God, who at sundry times and in divers manners

spake in time past unto the fathers by the prophets, hath in these last days spoken unto us by His Son, whom He hath appointed heir of all things, by whom also He made the worlds; who being the brightness of His glory, and the express image of His person, and upholding all things by the word of His power, when He had by Himself purged our sins, sat down on the right hand of the Majesty on high" (Heb. 1:1—3).

This passage suggests a process which ultimately reaches a climax, the process being that God "spake in times past"—i. e., throughout the Old Testament era—"in divers manners" (or *in different portions of the Scriptures*) given through the prophets from Genesis through Malachi.

For example, *to Adam* in the Garden of Eden God revealed the manner of the coming of the Lord Jesus Christ—He would be the seed of the woman (Gen. 3:15).

To Abraham God revealed that Christ would be from the nation of which Abraham was the head: "Now the Lord had said unto Abram, Get thee out of thy country, and from thy kindred, and from thy father's house, unto a land that I will shew thee: and I will make of thee a great nation, and I will bless thee, and make thy name great; and thou shalt be a blessing: and I will bless them that bless thee, and curse him that curseth thee: and *in thee shall all families of the earth be blessed*" (Gen. 12:1—3).

To Jacob God revealed that Christ would be of the tribe of Judah: "The sceptre *shall not depart from Judah,* nor a lawgiver from between his feet, *until Shiloh come;* and unto Him shall the gathering of the people be" (Gen. 49:10).

To Micah God revealed that Christ would be born

35

in the obscure village of Bethlehem: "Thou, Bethlehem Ephratah, though thou be little among the thousands of Judah, yet *out of thee shall He come forth unto me that is to be Ruler in Israel;* whose goings forth have been from of old, from everlasting" (Micah 5:2).

To Malachi God revealed that Christ's coming would be heralded by a forerunner: *"Behold, I will send my messenger, and he shall prepare the way before me:* and the Lord, whom ye seek, shall suddenly come to His temple, even the messenger of the covenant, whom ye delight in: behold, He shall come, saith the Lord of hosts" (Mal. 3:1).

To Daniel God revealed that when Christ should appear He would be "cut off" at the end of the sixty-ninth week of the seventy weeks of prophetic years: "And *after threescore and two weeks shall Messiah be cut off, but not for Himself:* and the people of the prince that shall come shall destroy the city and the sanctuary; and the end thereof shall be with a flood, and unto the end of the war desolations are determined" (Dan. 9:26).

To Zechariah God revealed that Christ would be betrayed and sold for the price of a slave—thirty pieces of silver: "And the Lord said unto me, Cast it unto the potter: a goodly price that I was prised at of them. And I took *the thirty pieces of silver,* and cast them to the potter in the house of the Lord" (Zech. 11:13).

To Isaiah God revealed that Christ would die for the sins of the people, that He would be numbered with the transgressors, that He would intercede for His murderers, and that He would be buried in the grave of a rich man:

"He made His grave with the wicked, and *with*

36

the rich in His death; because He had done no violence, neither was any deceit in His mouth. Yet it pleased the Lord to bruise Him; He hath put Him to grief: when thou shalt make His soul an offering for sin, He shall see His seed, He shall prolong His days, and the pleasure of the Lord shall prosper in His hand. He shall see of the travail of His soul, and shall be satisfied: by His knowledge shall my righteous servant justify many; for *He shall bear their iniquities.* Therefore will I divide Him a portion with the great, and He shall divide the spoil with the strong; because He hath poured out His soul unto death: and *He was numbered with the transgressors; and He bare the sin of many, and made intercession for the transgressors"* (Isa. 53:9—12).

To David God revealed that Christ would be of the house and lineage of David: "The Lord hath sworn in truth unto David; He will not turn from it: *Of the fruit of thy body will I set upon thy throne"* (Psalm 132:11).

Also to David God revealed that Christ would die by crucifixion: "I am poured out like water, and all my bones are out of joint: my heart is like wax; it is melted in the midst of my bowels. My strength is dried up like a potsherd; and my tongue cleaveth to my jaws; and thou hast brought me into the dust of death. For dogs have compassed me: the assembly of the wicked have inclosed me: *they pierced my hands and my feet.* I may tell all my bones: they look and stare upon me. They part my garments among them, and cast lots upon my vesture" (Psalm 22:14—18).

Death by crucifixion was not a custom of the *Jews*— they *stoned* people to death. Only godless Rome decreed such a horribly cruel way to put men to death.

Crucifixion was one of the most painful, inhuman ways ever devised as a means of execution. Psalm 22, given by divine inspiration and written centuries before the birth of Jesus, paints a complete and horrible picture of death by crucifixion—at that time unknown to the human family.

It was *also to David* that God revealed that Christ would rise from the dead: "For *thou wilt not leave my soul in hell:* neither wilt thou suffer thine Holy One to see corruption. *Thou wilt shew me the path of life:* in thy presence is fulness of joy; at thy right hand there are pleasures for evermore" (Psalm 16:10, 11).

Thus in these "divers portions" of Old Testament Scripture God made known His purpose regarding the Lord Jesus Christ, but Christ Himself when He came was the *culmination* of these revelations. He was the fulfillment of *all Old Testament prophecies* concerning His first advent. He was the fulfillment of every jot and tittle of the *law*—the end of the law to all who believe (Rom. 10:4). He fulfilled every *holy day*, every *offering*, every *type* set forth in the Old Testament. Therefore the Word of God is complete; He has said all there is *to be said* insofar as salvation, life eternal, and godliness are concerned.

The Old Testament Is Inspired
As Surely As the New Testament Is Inspired

"All Scripture is given by inspiration of God, and is profitable for doctrine, for reproof, for correction, for instruction in righteousness: that the man of God may be perfect, throughly furnished unto all good works" (II Tim. 3:16, 17).

"We have also a more sure word of prophecy; whereunto ye do well that ye take heed, as unto a light that shineth in a dark place, until the day dawn, and the day star arise in your hearts: knowing this first, that no prophecy of the Scripture is of any private interpretation. *For the prophecy came not in old time by the will of man: but holy men of God spake as they were moved by the Holy Ghost"* (II Pet. 1:19—21).

I emphasize these facts of divine foreshadowing and prophecy because in these days of liberalism and modernism thousands of men boldly *deny* the inspiration of the Old Testament. They would have us believe that its wonderful prophecies are only human predictions, that they are of human origin, and therefore they should be accepted as legend rather than fact.

By denying the revelation of God in the Old Testament Scriptures these men also deny *the Son of God* and His work—the divinely declared fact that we are God's purchased possession, bought with the precious blood of His only begotten Son: "But there were false prophets also among the people, even as there shall be *false teachers* among you, who privily shall bring in damnable heresies, *even denying the Lord that bought them* and bring upon themselves swift destruction. And *many shall follow their pernicious ways;* by reason of whom the Way of Truth shall be evil spoken of" (II Pet. 2:1, 2).

According to the Word of God, those who deny the Old Testament prophecies concerning the coming of Christ and His work are definitely *antichrists:* "Little children, it is the last time: and as ye have heard that antichrist shall come, *even now* are there *many antichrists;* whereby we know that it is the last time" (I John 2:18).

So we see that even in John's day there were apostate teachers—and he referred to them as *"antichrists."*

39

The apostate teachers of today, the liberals and modernists, deny the written Word of God. They say that *part* of our Bible is the Word of God, but *only part* of it. However, I declare dogmatically and without apology or reservation that our Bible is God-breathed—from the first word in Genesis to the last word in Revelation! The Bible does not simply *contain* the Word of God, *it IS the Word of God;* and the Bible is *ALL there is* of the Word of God, recorded for our admonition. There are no "lost" books of God's Word, there are no *additional* books.

The so-called "higher criticism" of today is the leaven of Satan which leavens many of the theological schools of Christendom. Big denominational seminaries and schools of theology teach young men to *deny* the Word of God instead of doing as Paul did in commanding young Timothy to *"preach the WORD"* (II Tim. 4:2). Paul also warned Timothy, "The time will come when they will not endure sound doctrine; but after their own lusts shall they heap to themselves teachers, having itching ears; and they shall turn away their ears from the truth, and shall be turned unto fables" (II Tim. 4:3, 4). *We are living in that day of which Paul wrote!*

The system of Antichrist, anti-Christianity, denies the written Word of God and the Lord who bought them. Thus is this leaven of the modern Pharisees and Sadducees preparing an empty Christian profession for the reception of the Man of Sin, the Antichrist who will be revealed after the Rapture of the Church. It would be far more difficult for me to believe their Satanic teaching than it is for me to accept the Old Testament prophecies at face value as *"Thus saith the Lord!"* I confess that I do not *understand* all of God's Word, *but I BELIEVE it*—from the first verse of Gen-

40

esis through the last verse of Revelation!

The Incarnation of Christ, the Son of God

Let us turn now to the great truth of fundamental Christianity—the fact of the Incarnation of God's only begotten Son. In Genesis 3:15 the Seed of the woman was promised. In the fulness of time—God's own *appointed* time—the Son of God appeared on earth in the form of man: *"When the fulness of the time was come, God sent forth His Son,* made of a woman, made under the law, to redeem them that were under the law, that we might receive the adoption of sons" (Gal. 4:4, 5).

The Word which was in the beginning with God, that Word that *was God* and by whom all things were made, that same Word was made flesh and tabernacled among men on earth:

"In the beginning was the Word, and the Word was with God, and the Word was God. The same was in the beginning with God. All things were made by Him; and without Him was not any thing made that was made. . . . And the Word was made flesh, and dwelt among us, (and we beheld His glory, the glory as of the only begotten of the Father,) full of grace and truth. . . . No man hath seen God at any time; the only begotten Son, which is in the bosom of the Father, He hath declared Him" (John 1:1—18 in part).

Christ subsisted in the form of God; yet He emptied Himself, took upon Him the form of a servant, and was made in the likeness of men, that in a body of humiliation He might know life as *we* know life, He might be tempted in all points as we are, and remain sinless:

"We see Jesus, who was made a little lower than

41

the angels for the suffering of death, crowned with glory and honour; that He by the grace of God should taste death for every man. For it became Him, for whom are all things, and by whom are all things, in bringing many sons unto glory, to make the Captain of their salvation perfect through sufferings. For both He that sanctifieth and they who are sanctified are all of one: for which cause He is not ashamed to call them brethren, saying, I will declare thy name unto my brethren, in the midst of the Church will I sing praise unto thee. And again, I will put my trust in Him. And again, Behold I and the children which God hath given me.

"Forasmuch then as the children are partakers of flesh and blood, He also Himself likewise took part of the same; that through death He might destroy him that had the power of death, that is, the devil; and deliver them who through fear of death were all their lifetime subject to bondage. For verily He took not on Him the nature of angels; but He took on Him the seed of Abraham. Wherefore in all things it behoved Him to be made like unto His brethren, that He might be a merciful and faithful High Priest in things pertaining to God, to make reconciliation for the sins of the people. For in that He Himself hath suffered being tempted, He is able to succour them that are tempted" (Heb. 2:9–18).

"For we have not an High Priest which cannot be touched with the feeling of our infirmities; but was *in all points tempted like as we are, YET WITHOUT SIN*" (Heb. 4:15).

The Incarnation is a mystery, the depths of which human reason has never fathomed—*nor ever will!* We must approach the subject in a spirit of reverence and deep humility, for like Moses before the burning bush *we stand on holy ground.*

Jesus was the *God-Man.* He was truly God, but He was just as truly man, made *"like unto His brethren" in all things.* He is called *"the Son of man"* more than seventy-five times in the New Testament, and that name was applied to Him not only while He was on earth, but also after He ascended back to the Father and took His place at the right hand of God on the throne.

In Romans 3:23 we read, *"ALL have sinned,* and come short of the glory of God," and Romans 6:23 tells us, *"The wages of sin is DEATH."* Therefore, if sinners were to be saved from eternal damnation it was necessary that a qualified substitute be found to die in the sinner's place! It was also necessary that that substitute be sinless, yet that He be tempted in all points as we are tempted in order that He might know the feeling of our infirmities, our human frailties, that He might become our faithful and compassionate High Priest.

Since the character and nature of God demanded that our substitute be righteous, holy, sinless, undefiled and untouched by evil or iniquity, *only God* could *provide* such a substitute. God's Christ perfectly fulfilled all of these qualifications; but God cannot die (Psalm 90:1, 2), nor can God be tempted with evil (James 1:13). The substitute must be flesh as man is flesh, made in the likeness of man. Therefore the Word, God's Christ, was made flesh in order that *we* might be made acceptable to God in Christ:

"Having predestinated us unto the adoption of children by Jesus Christ to Himself, according to the good pleasure of His will, to the praise of the glory of His grace, *wherein He hath made us accepted IN THE BELOVED"* (Eph. 1:5, 6).

John, that disciple whom Jesus loved, penned the message for this day and hour. In I John 1:1—4 we read:

"That which was from the beginning, which we have heard, which we have seen with our eyes, which we have looked upon, and our hands have handled, of the Word of life; (For the life was manifested, and we have seen it, and bear witness, and shew unto you that eternal life, which was with the Father, and was manifested unto us;) That which we have seen and heard declare we unto you, that ye also may have fellowship with us: and truly our fellowship is with the Father, and with His Son Jesus Christ. And these things write we unto you, that your joy may be full."

Now shall we examine this passage a bit more closely? John says, *"That which was from the beginning . . . ."* In the beginning was the Word, the Word was Jesus; so "that which was from the beginning" speaks of Jesus, the living Word.

". . . which we have heard . . . ." John heard Jesus preach and teach, he walked and talked with the Lord for three and one-half years. He had not the slightest doubt of that which he heard, because "faith cometh by hearing, and hearing by the Word of God" (Rom. 10:17).

". . . which we have seen with our eyes . . . ." John saw Jesus in the flesh, he *"looked upon"* Him—that is, he *gazed* upon Him, not in a casual way, but intently, raptly.

". . . and our hands have handled . . . ." If there had been any room for doubt as to what he had heard and seen, the *sense of touch* removed it. The Word was tangible. John had not only touched the Lord, he had leaned on His breast at the Last Supper (John 13:25).

44

"*. . . of the Word of Life.*" The Word was alive in the beginning, but two thousand years ago the Word that was in the beginning took the form of human life. *The Word IS life*—and *through the Word* God created all things that are created, in heaven and in earth. Thus "*the Life was manifested,*" and John declares, "We have *seen* it, and *bear witness,* and shew *unto you* that eternal life, which was with the Father, and was manifested unto us."

Thus "*we see Jesus*"—that is, we believe the message God gave concerning His Son, and with the eye of the inner man, the eye of faith, *we see Him.* We have not seen Him as *John* saw Him, but we know He is everything John declared Him to be, that our joy might be full. We know Jesus lived, that He was God in flesh, that He was tempted in all points as we are tempted, yet without sin. We know that He conquered the world, the flesh, and the devil, death, hell, and the grave. We know this because *the Word of God declares it and "through FAITH we understand!*" (Heb. 11:3).

Peter speaks of "Jesus Christ, whom *having not seen, ye love;* in whom, though now ye see Him not, yet believing, ye rejoice with joy unspeakable and full of glory" (I Pet. 1:8).

Jesus was made "a little lower than the angels," He was made "like unto His brethren," *that He might suffer death*—and when He came into the world He knew exactly why He came. He came to lay His life down that *we* might have life and have it abundantly.

From Hebrews 2:14 we learn more about *the human nature* of the Lamb of God: "Forasmuch then as the children are partakers of flesh and blood, He also Himself likewise *took part of the same . . . .*" As our own children are partakers of our flesh and blood, Jesus

45

"took part of the same"—that is, He took the *flesh* part of man and was made like unto sinful flesh. Thus He received His flesh from the Virgin Mary; but the life of the flesh is in the blood (Lev. 17:14), and His blood was the blood of God (Acts 20:28). God purchased the Church with His own blood, therefore the blood of Jesus was the blood of God.

The Son of God took flesh in order that He might die, and in that body of flesh He did what the law could never have done. He fulfilled every jot and tittle of the law, every demand of God's righteousness and holiness. Now God can be just, and yet justify the ungodly:

"But now the righteousness of God without the law is manifested, being witnessed by the law and the prophets; even the righteousness of God which is by faith of Jesus Christ unto all and upon all them that believe: for there is no difference: for all have sinned, and come short of the glory of God; being justified freely by His grace through the redemption that is in Christ Jesus: whom God hath set forth to be a propitiation through faith in His blood, to declare His righteousness for the remission of sins that are past, through the forbearance of God; to declare, I say, at this time His righteousness: *that He might be JUST, and the JUSTIFIER of him which believeth in Jesus.* Where is boasting then? It is excluded. By what law? of works? Nay: but by the law of faith. *Therefore we conclude that a man is justified by faith without the deeds of the law*" (Rom. 3:21—28).

Today there is a Man in heaven: "For there is one God, and one Mediator between God and men, *the MAN Christ Jesus*" (I Tim. 2:5). It is indeed a grave and dangerous thing to deny the reality of Christ's body of flesh.

Past: The Incarnation

In I John 4:1—3 we read, "Beloved, believe not every spirit, but *try* the spirits whether they are of God: because many false prophets are gone out into the world. *Hereby know ye the Spirit of God:* Every spirit that confesseth that Jesus Christ is come *in the flesh* is of God: and every spirit that *confesseth not* that Jesus Christ is come in the flesh is not of God: and this is that spirit of Antichrist, whereof ye have heard that it should come; and even now already is it in the world."

Even after His resurrection the body of Jesus was a body of flesh and bones. He gave His blood that we might have life, but when He appeared to the disciples in the upper room He invited them, "Behold my hands and my feet, that it is I myself: *handle me, and see; for a spirit hath not FLESH AND BONES, as ye see me have.* And when He had thus spoken, He shewed them His hands and His feet. And while they yet believed not for joy, and wondered, He said unto them, *Have ye here any meat?* And they gave Him a piece of a broiled fish, and of an honeycomb. *And He took it, AND DID EAT BEFORE THEM"* (Luke 24:39—43).

We note that on occasion, even while Jesus tabernacled in His body of flesh, His divine glory broke through and some of His disciples beheld that glory. Three of the Gospel writers record one event when Peter, James, and John were with Jesus on the Mount of Transfiguration and He was transfigured before them:

Matthew tells us, "After six days Jesus taketh Peter, James, and John his brother, and bringeth them up into an high mountain apart, and was transfigured before them: and His face did shine as the sun, and His raiment was white as the light. And, behold,

47

there appeared unto them Moses and Elias talking with Him" (Matt. 17:1—3).

Mark records the same incident in these words: "After six days Jesus taketh with Him Peter, and James, and John, and leadeth them up into an high mountain apart by themselves: and He was transfigured before them. And His raiment became shining, exceeding white as snow; so as no fuller on earth can white them. And there appeared unto them Elias with Moses: and they were talking with Jesus" (Mark 9:2—4).

Luke tells us that Jesus took Peter and John and James, "and went up into a mountain to pray. And as He prayed, the fashion of His countenance was altered, and His raiment was white and glistering. And, behold, there talked with Him two men, which were Moses and Elias: who appeared in glory, and spake of His decease which He should accomplish at Jerusalem" (Luke 9:28—31).

Stephen saw the risen Christ, *the MAN Christ Jesus,* standing at the right hand of God. We read his words in Acts 7:55, 56 as he was being stoned to death for his testimony: "But he, being full of the Holy Ghost, looked up stedfastly into heaven, and saw the glory of God, and Jesus standing on the right hand of God, and said, *Behold, I see the heavens opened, and THE SON OF MAN standing on the right hand of God.*"

John the Beloved saw the Lamb of God, *the Man Christ Jesus,* who is even now at the right hand of God interceding for us. John wrote, "I beheld, and, lo, in the midst of the throne and of the four beasts, and in the midst of the elders, stood *a Lamb as it had been SLAIN,* having seven horns and seven eyes, which are the seven Spirits of God sent forth into all the earth" (Rev. 5:6).

48

Jesus Himself testified before His enemies, "Hereafter shall ye see *the Son of man* sitting on the right hand of power, *and coming in the clouds of heaven*" (Matt. 26:64).   Yes, *the MAN Christ Jesus—the same Man in the same body*—will return to this earth just as He went away.   This fundamental truth is clearly declared in God's Word:

"And when He (Jesus) had spoken these things, while they (the disciples) beheld, *He was taken up; and A CLOUD received Him out of their sight.*   And while they looked stedfastly toward heaven as He went up, behold, two men stood by them in white apparel; which also said: Ye men of Galilee, why stand ye gazing up into heaven?   *This same Jesus, which is taken up from you into heaven, shall so come IN LIKE MANNER as ye have seen Him go into heaven*" (Acts 1:9—11).

Yes, Jesus will return in the clouds—the same Man in the same glorified body in which He ascended from the Mount of Olives as His disciples gazed after Him. There is a Man in heaven now. He is our Redeemer— we are saved from the *penalty* of sin through His sacrifice on Calvary.   He is our Saviour—we are daily saved from the *power* of sin. He is our *Mediator*—the propitiation for our sins, seated at the right hand of God where He ever makes intercession for us.   And— glory to His precious name—He is our soon-coming King!

The Word of God declares that Jesus will come in the clouds to call His own to meet Him in the air: *"The Lord Himself* shall descend from heaven with a shout, with the voice of the archangel, and with the trump of God: and the dead in Christ shall rise first: then we which are alive and remain shall be caught up together with them in the clouds, to meet the Lord

in the air: and so shall we ever be with the Lord"
(I Thess. 4:16, 17).

At that time (also declared in the Word of God),
Christ will *"change* our vile body, that it may be
fashioned *like unto His glorious body,* according to
the working whereby He is able even to subdue all
things unto Himself" (Phil. 3:21).

John the Beloved declares, "Beloved, *NOW are we
the sons of God,* and it doth not yet appear what we
shall be: but we know that, when He shall appear,
we shall be LIKE HIM; for we shall see Him as He
is" (I John 3:2).

In I Corinthians 15:49 the Apostle Paul tells us,
"As we have borne the image of the earthy, *we shall
also bear the image of the heavenly."*

Just as the Scriptures teach the *Divinity* of Jesus,
they also teach the *humanity* of Jesus. He was human
as *we* are human—except for His sinlessness. He was
of the seed of David *according to the flesh.* The Virgin Mary was as truly the mother of Jesus as the dear
woman who gave me birth is my mother. The Holy
Ghost overshadowed Mary, the power of the Highest
came upon her, she conceived and brought forth the
only begotten Son of God. I repeat—Jesus was of the
seed of David, of the tribe of Judah—*very MAN;* but
He was also *very GOD!*

The Incarnation Announced

"And in the sixth month the angel Gabriel was sent
from God unto a city of Galilee, named Nazareth, to
a virgin espoused to a man whose name was Joseph,
of the house of David; and the virgin's name was
Mary. And the angel came in unto her, and said,
Hail, thou that art highly favoured, the Lord is with
thee: blessed art thou among women.

Past: The Incarnation

"And when she saw him, she was troubled at his saying, and cast in her mind what manner of salutation this should be. And the angel said unto her, Fear not, Mary: for thou hast found favour with God. And, behold, thou shalt conceive in thy womb, and bring forth a son, and shalt call His name JESUS. He shall be great, and shall be called the Son of the Highest: and the Lord God shall give unto Him the throne of His father David: and He shall reign over the house of Jacob for ever; and of His kingdom there shall be no end.

"Then said Mary unto the angel, How shall this be, seeing I know not a man? And the angel answered and said unto her, The Holy Ghost shall come upon thee, and the power of the Highest shall overshadow thee: therefore also that holy thing which shall be born of thee shall be called the Son of God" (Luke 1:26—35).

Notice: *"The HOLY GHOST shall come upon thee . . . The power of THE HIGHEST shall overshadow thee. Therefore . . . that HOLY THING which shall be born of thee shall be called THE SON OF GOD!"* Because the human nature of Christ was thus produced, it was a nature without sin. He was born in a body of flesh like unto our bodies—but He was without sin. He was absolutely holy, absolutely righteous and sinless because He was conceived by the Holy Ghost.

The Incarnation did not *make* Christ God's Son— He was *ever* the Son of God. He was with God in the beginning. Therefore the Scripture here says, *He "shall be CALLED the Son of God,"* God manifested in flesh, and that is *precisely what Jesus was* in His body of humiliation.

There are those who say they cannot accept the

51

fact of the Incarnation, they cannot accept the fact that Christ was God in flesh, born of a virgin with God Almighty as His Father. They say this cannot be *explained,* therefore it cannot be understood, and they refuse to accept what they cannot comprehend! Beloved, if I could comprehend or explain how Jesus Christ was both God and man, I would be ashamed to publicly announce Jesus as my Saviour because He would be no greater than I.

The Incarnation *cannot* be explained by finite minds. No mortal mind can fathom the depths of that mystery and fully grasp the wonderful personality of Christ the God-Man. The Lord Jesus Christ cannot be explained by means of man's language, through man's wisdom, or in man's laboratories. It is far, far better to abide by the simple statements and declarations of the Word of God than to enter into numerous speculations which can never solve the mystery of the Incarnation.

We are *saved* by grace *through FAITH,* the just shall *live by faith,* and *"whatsoever is NOT of faith is SIN"* (Rom. 14:23). Therefore *"Through FAITH we understand"* (Heb. 11:3) — through faith we accept the Word of God concerning God's love and Christ's coming into the world. I believe John 3:16. I believe "God so loved the world that He gave His only begotten Son" — and I believe God's only begotten Son willingly left the glories of heaven and took a body of humiliation that He might taste death for all men. I believe Christ emptied Himself of His outward glory, to appear in the form of man. This does not mean that He emptied Himself of His glory as the second Person in the Godhead, but He laid aside His outward glory and came into this world, born of the Virgin Mary who wrapped Him in swaddling clothes and laid Him in a manger. He who rested on the bosom of the Virgin is the One who was in the bosom of the Father in the beginning (John 1:1, 14, 18).

I also believe that these truths, declared in God's Word but beyond the comprehension of the human intellect, should rest on Deuteronomy 29:29:

"The SECRET THINGS belong unto the Lord our God: but those things which are revealed belong unto us and to our children for ever, that we may do all the words of this law."*

Christ's Incarnation Is the Foundation of the Gospel Message

Upon the fact of the Incarnation rests the entire Gospel message, from Genesis 3:15 through Revelation 22:21! If there *was* no incarnation, if Christ *did not* become man, then we have no Gospel, no God, no Bible and no hope! If Jesus was not born of a virgin, then He was born of a harlot. If He was not conceived as the Bible records, then He was conceived out of wedlock—weak humanity, conceived in sin and born of iniquity. How could such a one be the Saviour of sinners?

Those who deny the virgin birth of Jesus have no right to call themselves Christians. The sad situation today is that the Incarnation is not denied by confirmed atheists and infidels alone, but by thousands of *churchmen* who go into the pulpit on Sunday morning and deny the virgin birth, the Incarnation, the shed blood of Calvary, and other fundamentals of the faith—and they do it in the name of "religion," garbed in their religious best and parading as ministers of the Gospel!

Equally sad is the fact that many born again believers are members of churches pastored by just such men and support them with their presence, their prayers, and their money. Every Christian who attends a church where a liberal or modernist is pastor should immediately withdraw from that assembly and seek a church where God's man gives out God's message. Do I have Scripture for such a statement? I certainly do! In II John 9—11 God's Word expressly declares:

"Whosoever transgresseth, and abideth not in the doctrine of Christ, hath not God. He that abideth in the doctrine of Christ, he hath both the Father and the Son. *If there come any unto you, and bring not this doctrine, receive him not into your house, neither bid him God speed:* FOR HE THAT BIDDETH HIM GOD SPEED IS PARTAKER OF HIS EVIL DEEDS!"

Surely the end of the age is upon us! The Word of God clearly teaches that a rejection of the fundamentals of the faith will occur just before the Lord's second coming. Liberalism and modernism are not on the decline. They are swiftly advancing, and as the end approaches "evil men and seducers shall wax worse and worse, deceiving, and being deceived" (II Tim. 3:13). I am not a pessimist, I am not a calamity howler; but I do believe the Bible. Therefore I know that world conditions are not going to improve. On the contrary, they will grow progressively worse until God says, "It is enough!"

The Purpose of Christ's Incarnation

Through the Incarnation, the invisible God (the Eternal Spirit whom no man has seen) was *made known* to man. I cannot *comprehend* the Eternal Spirit—Jehovah God who had no beginning. God has *always been*, He is from everlasting to everlasting. My finite mind cannot grasp the understanding of such a

54

Being—but I *can* comprehend a Baby born two thousand years ago, a Baby named Jesus; and by faith I can understand that through the miraculous power of Almighty God that Baby was born of the Virgin Mary.

John 1:18 declares, *"No man* hath seen *God* at any time; the only begotten *Son,* which is in the *bosom of the Father, He hath DECLARED HIM."* The Lord Jesus Christ is the image of the invisible God (Col. 1:15). He is one with the Father, therefore He could truthfully say, *"He that hath seen ME hath seen the FATHER"* (John 14:9).

The attributes of God were clearly made known in the Incarnation. We behold the holiness of God in the holy life of Jesus on earth. We find the omniscience of God in the fact that Jesus knew what was in men, He knew what they were thinking: "Jesus did not commit Himself unto them, because He knew all men, and needed not that any should testify of man: for He knew what was in man" (John 2:24, 25).

When Jesus healed a man sick of the palsy, He simply said to the man, "Son, be of good cheer; thy sins be forgiven thee." But "certain of the scribes said *within themselves,* This Man blasphemeth! *And Jesus KNOWING THEIR THOUGHTS said,* Wherefore think ye evil in your hearts? For whether is easier, to say, Thy sins be forgiven thee; or to say, Arise, and walk?" (Matt. 9:2—5).

In Matthew 12:24, 25 the Pharisees accused Jesus of casting out devils by Beelzebub, prince of devils. *"And JESUS KNEW THEIR THOUGHTS,* and said unto them, Every kingdom divided against itself is brought to desolation; and every city or house divided against itself shall not stand."

Jesus manifested the *power* of Almighty God in controlling the forces of nature, commanding the wind and the waves to be still:

"And the same day, when the even was come, He saith unto them, Let us pass over unto the other side. And when they had sent away the multitude, they took Him even as He was in the ship. And there were also with Him other little ships. And there arose a great storm of wind, and the waves beat into the ship, so that it was now full. And He was in the hinder part of the ship, asleep on a pillow: and they awake Him, and say unto Him, Master, carest thou not that we perish?

"And He arose, and rebuked the wind, and said unto the sea, Peace, be still! And the wind ceased, and there was a great calm. And He said unto them, Why are ye so fearful? How is it that ye have no faith? And they feared exceedingly, and said one to another, *What manner of Man is this, that even the wind and the sea obey Him?"* (Mark 4:35—41).

At a wedding feast in Cana, He turned water into wine. When the supply of wine was exhausted, He said to the servants of the house, *"Fill the waterpots with water.* And they filled them up to the brim. And He saith unto them, *Draw out now, and bear unto the governor of the feast.* And they bare it. When the ruler of the feast had tasted the water that was made wine, and knew not whence it was: (but the servants which drew the water knew;) the governor of the feast called the bridegroom, and saith unto him, Every man at the beginning doth set forth good wine; and when men have well drunk, then that which is worse: but thou hast kept the good wine until now. *This beginning of miracles did Jesus in Cana of Galilee, and manifested forth His glory;* and His disciples believed on Him" (John 2:7—11).

Jesus manifested *the love and compassion* of Almighty God for suffering humanity when He healed all manner of diseases, cast out demons, and restored the dead to life. In Matthew 9:35, 36 we read, "Jesus went about all the cities and villages, teaching in their synagogues, and preaching the Gospel of the kingdom, *and healing every sickness and every disease among the people.* But when He saw the multitudes, *He was moved with compassion on them,* because they fainted, and were scattered abroad, as sheep having no shepherd."

Mark records the following account of Christ's healing of the maniac of Gadara:

"And they came over unto the other side of the sea, into the country of the Gadarenes. And when He was come out of the ship, immediately there met Him out of the tombs a man with an unclean spirit, who had his dwelling among the tombs; and no man could bind him, no, not with chains: because that he had been often bound with fetters and chains, and the chains had been plucked asunder by him, and the fetters broken in pieces: neither could any man tame him. And always, night and day, he was in the mountains, and in the tombs, crying, and cutting himself with stones. *But when he saw Jesus afar off, he ran and worshipped Him,* and cried with a loud voice, and said, What have I to do with thee, Jesus, thou Son of the most high God? I adjure thee by God, that thou torment me not.

"For He said unto him, Come out of the man, thou unclean spirit. And He asked him, What is thy name? And he answered, saying, My name is Legion: for we are many. And he besought Him much that He would not send them away out of the country.

"Now there was there nigh unto the mountains a great herd of swine feeding. And all the devils besought Him,

57

saying, Send us into the swine, that we may enter into them. And forthwith Jesus gave them leave. And the unclean spirits went out, and entered into the swine: and the herd ran violently down a steep place into the sea, (they were about two thousand;) and were choked in the sea. And they that fed the swine fled, and told it in the city, and in the country. And they went out to see what it was that was done.

"And they come to Jesus, and see him that was possessed with the devil, and had the legion, sitting, and clothed, and in his right mind: and they were afraid. And they that saw it told them how it befell to him that was possessed with the devil, and also concerning the swine. And they began to pray Him to depart out of their coasts.

"And when He was come into the ship, he that had been possessed with the devil prayed Him that he might be with Him. Howbeit Jesus suffered him not, but saith unto him, *Go home to thy friends, and tell them how great things the Lord hath done for thee, and hath had compassion on thee"* (Mark 5:1−19).

In John 11:1−44 Jesus manifested *His power over death* when He called Lazarus forth from the grave. Mary and Martha sent word to Jesus that Lazarus was sick; but in spite of the Lord's love for these His dear friends, He did not go to Bethany until after Lazarus died. When He arrived in Bethany He inquired where Lazarus had been buried, He wept in sympathy for the two bereaved sisters, and when He reached the tomb of Lazarus he commanded that the stone be taken away from the door. Martha said to Him, *"Lord, by this time he stinketh: for he hath been dead FOUR DAYS.*

"Jesus saith unto her, *Said I not unto thee, that, if thou wouldest believe, thou shouldest see the glory of God?* Then they took away the stone from the place where the dead was laid. And Jesus lifted up His

58

eyes, and said, Father, I thank thee that thou hast heard me. And I knew that thou hearest me always: but because of the people which stand by I said it, that they may believe that thou hast sent me.

"And when He thus had spoken, *He cried with a loud voice, LAZARUS, COME FORTH!* And he that was dead came forth, bound hand and foot with grave-clothes: and his face was bound about with a napkin. *Jesus saith unto them, Loose him, and let him go!*"

In the Incarnation, the only begotten Son of God brought the *Word* of God to man. In Hebrews 1:1, 2 we read, "God, who at sundry times and in divers manners spake in time past unto the fathers by the prophets, *hath IN THESE LAST DAYS spoken unto us BY HIS SON*, whom He hath appointed heir of all things, by whom also He made the worlds."

In the Incarnation, the Lord Jesus Christ revealed the *will* of God. He made known God the Father, He made known the fact of eternal life, *abundant* life. He also made known the fact of the eternal, horrible *conscious suffering* and punishment of the wicked. During His earthly ministry He spoke words of prophecy concerning the great events of the future, events concerning Himself, His visible kingdom, and the end of the age when He should return to reign in righteousness forever.

The Incarnation was a divine imperative in anticipation of Christ's work as the Great High Priest of His people. After His crucifixion and resurrection He became our "merciful and faithful High Priest" (Heb. 2:17), and such He is *this very moment*. But all that He was to be, all that He is now—the last Adam, the head of the Church and of the new creation—this and much more *demanded* His Incarnation:

"Seeing then that we have a great High Priest, that

is passed into the heavens, Jesus the Son of God, let us hold fast our profession. For we have not an high priest which cannot be touched with the feeling of our infirmities; *but was in all points tempted like as we are, yet without sin.* Let us therefore come boldly unto the throne of grace, that we may obtain mercy, and find grace to help in time of need" (Heb. 4:14—16).

One Thing the Incarnation Could Not Accomplish

"As Moses lifted up the serpent in the wilderness, even so must the Son of man be lifted up: that whosoever believeth in Him should not perish, but have eternal life" (John 3:14, 15).

The great purpose of the Incarnation was Christ's work of redemption. It was for this great work that He came into the world. All else that He did—healing the sick, feeding the hungry, raising the dead—was incidental to redemption. John the Baptist expressed it in one brief sentence in John 1:29: *"Behold THE LAMB OF GOD, which taketh away the SIN of the world!"*

God hates sin. It was sin that demanded the death of God's only begotten Son on Calvary's cross. In the sight of God, sin is a curse which must be taken out of the way. *Propitiation* for sin had to be made before God could be just and yet justify the ungodly. Such propitiation demanded a sacrifice which would glorify and satisfy a holy God and also exalt God's righteousness. There was hostility between God and man, and it was necessary that *peace* be made. The full penalty of sin had to be borne, and the only One who could bear it was the only begotten Son of God. Therefore in order for Him to pay the sin-debt, His Incarnation was a divine imperative.

60

Past: The Incarnation

Christ's holy and sinless life on earth is marvelous, blessed, and glorious to read about. His loving words are words of comfort and joy, life and peace. His deeds of love—the cleansing of the lepers, the feeding of the five thousand, the deliverance of the man of Gadara, the healing of blind Bartimaeus—all are marvelous within themselves. The compassion He bestowed on suffering people is beyond real appreciation by finite beings. But *marvelous as all of these things were*, they could *never* have accomplished redemption nor paid the penalty for sin, they could never have provided redemption *for even one soul!*

The Incarnation brought God to man—but the Incarnation alone could never have brought man back to a holy and righteous God. The Incarnation alone could not have made an end to sin or made it possible for a righteous God to show mercy to fallen, hell-deserving sinners and still remain righteous. The great work of redemption could be accomplished only by the *death* of the Lamb of God on Calvary. It was imperative that the Son of man be lifted up as Moses had lifted up the brazen serpent in the wilderness, and Jesus declared, *"I, if I be lifted up from the earth, will draw all men unto me"* (John 12:32).

The Author and Prince of Life came that He might *give* His life a ransom for you, for me, for "whosoever will." He came "not to be ministered unto, but to minister, and to give His life a ransom for many" (Matt. 20:28), and only through His death could the great work of redemption be accomplished. There was no other way. He *must drink* the cup, drain it to the bitter dregs (John 18:11; Mark 10:38).

Christ's Work On the Cross and What It Accomplished

"Then the soldiers of the governor took Jesus into the

61

common hall, and gathered unto Him the whole band of soldiers. And they stripped Him, and put on Him a scarlet robe.
And when they had platted a crown of thorns, they put it
upon His head, and a reed in His right hand: and they bowed
the knee before Him, and mocked Him, saying, Hail, King
of the Jews!

"And they spit upon Him, and took the reed, and smote
Him on the head. And after that they had mocked Him, they
took the robe off from Him, and put His own raiment on
Him, and led Him away to crucify Him. And as they came
out, they found a man of Cyrene, Simon by name: him they
compelled to bear His cross.

"And when they were come unto a place called Golgotha,
that is to say, a place of a skull, they gave Him vinegar to
drink mingled with gall: and when He had tasted thereof, He
would not drink. And they crucified Him, and parted His
garments, casting lots: that it might be fulfilled which was
spoken by the prophet, They parted my garments among them,
and upon my vesture did they cast lots.

"And sitting down they watched Him there; and set up
over His head His accusation written, THIS IS JESUS THE
KING OF THE JEWS. Then were there two thieves crucified
with Him, one on the right hand, and another on the left.
And they that passed by reviled Him, wagging their heads,
and saying, Thou that destroyest the temple, and buildest it
in three days, save thyself. If thou be the Son of God, come
down from the cross.

"Likewise also the chief priests mocking Him, with the
scribes and elders, said, He saved others; Himself He cannot
save. If He be the King of Israel, let Him now come down
from the cross, and we will believe Him. He trusted in God;
let Him deliver Him now, if He will have Him: for He said,
I am the Son of God. The thieves also, which were crucified
with Him, cast the same in His teeth.

"Now from the sixth hour there was darkness over all the

land unto the ninth hour. And about the ninth hour Jesus cried with a loud voice, saying, Eli, Eli, lama sabachthani? that is to say, My God, my God, why hast thou forsaken me? Some of them that stood there, when they heard that, said, This Man calleth for Elias. And straightway one of them ran, and took a spunge, and filled it with vinegar, and put it on a reed, and gave Him to drink. The rest said, Let be, let us see whether Elias will come to save Him.

"Jesus, when He had cried again with a loud voice, yielded up the ghost. And, behold, the veil of the temple was rent in twain from the top to the bottom; and the earth did quake, and the rocks rent; and the graves were opened; and many bodies of the saints which slept arose, and came out of the graves after His resurrection, and went into the holy city, and appeared unto many.

"Now when the centurion, and they that were with Him, watching Jesus, saw the earthquake, and those things that were done, they feared greatly, saying, TRULY THIS WAS THE SON OF GOD!" (Matt. 27:27—54).

What mortal tongue or pen could possibly describe the heart-breaking yet most glorious truth of the only begotten Son of God dying for the ungodly—the Just One dying for the unjust? Peter wrote, "For even hereunto were ye called: because Christ also suffered for us, leaving us an example, that ye should follow His steps: who did no sin, neither was guile found in His mouth: who, when He was reviled, reviled not again; when He suffered, He threatened not; but committed Himself to Him that judgeth righteously: *who His own self bare our sins in His own body on the tree, that we, being dead to sins, should live unto righteousness: by whose stripes ye were healed.* For ye were as sheep going astray; but are now returned unto the Shepherd and Bishop of your souls" (I Pet. 2:21—25).

In I Peter 3:18 we read, "For Christ also hath *once suffered for sins, the Just for the unjust,* that He might bring us to God, being put to death in the flesh, but quickened by the Spirit."

Who could begin to estimate the eternal results of Christ's work on the cross, when God made Him to be sin for us, He who knew no sin, "that we might be made the righteousness of God in Him" (II Cor. 5:21). No mortal will ever touch the hem of the garment when it comes to understanding the spiritual depths of Calvary where Jesus died to take away our sins and make possible our salvation. Each time we look at Calvary we learn something new, something rich that we have never seen before; but we can *never* know what Christ's death on the cross meant for *Him,* nor can we ever know, even to a small degree, what His death meant to God the Eternal Father!

Christ Made Sin For Us

"For the law having a shadow of good things to come, and not the very image of the things, can never with those sacrifices which they offered year by year continually make the comers thereunto perfect. For then would they not have ceased to be offered? because that the worshippers once purged should have had no more conscience of sins. But in those sacrifices there is a remembrance again made of sins every year. *For it is not possible that the blood of bulls and of goats should take away sins.*

"Wherefore when He cometh into the world, He saith, Sacrifice and offering thou wouldest not, *but a BODY hast thou prepared me.* In burnt-offerings and sacrifices for sin thou hast had no pleasure. Then said I, *Lo, I come* (in the volume of the book it is written of me,) *to do thy will, O God.* Above when He said, Sacrifice and offering and burnt-offerings and offering for sin thou wouldest not, neither hadst pleasure therein; which are offered by the law. Then said He, Lo, I come to do thy will, O God. He taketh away the first, that He may establish the second. By the which will we are sanctified through the offering of the body of Jesus Christ once for all.

"And every priest standeth daily ministering and offering oftentimes the same sacrifices, which can never take away sins: *But THIS MAN, after He had offered ONE sacrifice for sins for ever, SAT DOWN ON THE RIGHT HAND OF GOD; from henceforth expecting till His enemies be made His footstool. For BY ONE OFFERING HE HATH PERFECTED FOR EVER THEM THAT ARE SANCTIFIED"* (Heb. 10:1—14).

The Levitical priests offered sacrifices year after year—often the same sacrifice for the same sins, over and over again. But those sacrifices could never take away sin—*"it is NOT POSSIBLE that the blood of bulls and of goats should take away sins."*

"Sacrifice and offering thou wouldest not, *but A BODY THOU HAST PREPARED ME."* God the Eternal Father prepared a body for Jesus. This puts before us the *indisputable, undeniable fact* of the Incarnation. Christ's body was a prepared body, holy and undefiled; a body in which sin could not dwell and on which death had no claim. "The wages of sin is *death"* (Rom. 6:23). *". . . Sin,* when it is finished, bringeth forth *death"* (James 1:15). But Jesus did not sin, there was no guile in Him. Therefore *death had no claim on Him.* But when He took the body God had prepared for Him, He said, *"Lo, I come to do THY WILL, O God . . .* By the which will *we* are sanctified through the offering of the body of Jesus Christ *once for all."*

"Christ being come an High Priest of good things to come, by a greater and more perfect tabernacle, not made with hands, that is to say, not of this building; neither by the blood of goats and calves, but by His own blood He entered in once into the holy place, having obtained eternal redemption for us. For if the blood of bulls and of goats, and the ashes of an heifer sprinkling the unclean, sanctifieth to the purifying of the flesh: how much MORE shall the blood of Christ, who through the Eternal Spirit offered Himself without spot to God, purge your conscience from dead works to serve the living God? And for this cause He is the Mediator of the New Testament, that by means of death, for the redemption of the transgressions that were under the first testament, they which are called might receive the promise of eternal inheritance" (Heb. 9:11—15).

Christ *"offered Himself WITHOUT SPOT to God."* The spotless Lamb of God, no spot or blemish upon Him, shed His precious blood on Calvary's cross in order to obtain redemption for you and for me. From "the beginning" God's Christ had pleased the Father in all things and had done God's will. As He witnessed to the Samaritan woman at Jacob's well, the disciples—knowing that He was tired and hungry— urged Him, *"Master, EAT."* He replied, "I have meat to eat that ye know not of. . . . *My meat is to do the will of Him that sent me,* and to finish His work" (John 4:31, 32, 34).

To God the Son, sin is as horrible and defiling as it is to God the Father. Yet such an One, holy and undefiled, was made to be sin for us. Christ had to stand in the place of all guilty sinners of all ages, while all the waves and billows of *divine wrath and judgment against sin* passed over Him! No other person has ever suffered—nor ever could suffer—as did the Man Christ Jesus. His suffering was in a way and to a degree impossible for us to understand—and He endured it all that you and I might not suffer in the lake of fire that burns with brimstone forever.

The Sufferings of Jesus

He suffered in Himself:—

"Now is my soul troubled; and what shall I say? Father, save me from this hour—but *for* this cause came I *unto this hour!*" (John 12:27). Christ looked toward Golgotha. Why His terrible agony in the Garden of Gethsemane? Why did His sweat become as it were great drops of blood falling to the ground? Why the repeated prayer, *"Father, if it be possible, let this cup PASS FROM ME"*? The answer is clear: He was bearing the sins of the whole world, the sin of every sinner from Adam to the last baby who will be born before the end of this age! Jesus took all sin of all ages and carried it to Calvary, there to nail it to the cross.

Just as no one else could pay the price of atonement for sin, so no one else can know the suffering Jesus knew; for His holy, righteous soul shrank from that which God hates as only He can hate—*sin*. In Gethsemane, Christ knew that He was about to be made sin for us, and He *knew* no sin. What suffering this fact produced in the Holy One of God, mere mortals can never know. It is beyond our imagination.

Christ suffered at the hands of men:—

"I gave my back to the smiters, and my cheeks to them that plucked off the hair: I hid not my face from shame and spitting" (Isa. 50:6).

"Who hath believed our report? and to whom is the arm of the Lord revealed? For He shall grow up before Him as a tender plant, and as a root out of a dry ground: He hath no form nor comeliness; and when we shall see Him, there is no beauty that we should desire Him. He is despised and rejected of men; a Man of sorrows, and acquainted with grief: and we hid as it were our faces from Him; He was despised, and we esteemed Him not.

"Surely He hath borne our griefs, and carried our sorrows: yet we did esteem Him stricken, smitten of God, and afflicted. But He was wounded for our transgressions, He was bruised for our iniquities: the chastisement of our peace was upon Him; and with His stripes we are healed. *ALL we like sheep have gone astray; we have turned every one to his own way; and the Lord hath laid on Him the iniquity of us ALL.*

"He was oppressed, and He was afflicted, yet He opened not His mouth: He is brought as a lamb to the slaughter, and as a sheep before her shearers is dumb, so He openeth not His mouth. He was taken from prison and from judgment: and who shall declare His generation? for He was cut off out of the land of the living: for the transgression of my people was He stricken. And He made His grave with the wicked, and with the rich in His death; because He had done no violence, neither was any deceit in His mouth.

"Yet it pleased the Lord to bruise Him; He hath put Him to grief: when thou shalt make His soul an offering for sin, He shall see His seed, He shall prolong His days, and the pleasure of the Lord shall prosper in His hand. He shall see of the travail of His soul, and shall be satisfied: by His knowledge shall my righteous servant justify many; for He shall bear their iniquities. Therefore will I divide Him a portion with the great, and He shall divide the spoil with the strong; because He hath poured out His soul unto death: and He was numbered with the transgressors; and He bare the sin of many, and made intercession for the transgressors" (Isa. 53:1—12).

All the wickedness, vileness, and cruelty of which

man is capable was brought out and spent on the blessed Son of God, the sacrificial Lamb who willingly came to lay His life down for the sin of mankind. How His sensitive, holy soul and body must have quivered under the whipping, the buffeting, the spitting, the mocking, and the shame of the cross! God's Word plainly tells us that *Jesus despised the shame of the cross*—but He endured it "for the joy that was set before Him," the joy at the right hand of the throne of God (Heb. 12:2). Yet even as they crucified Him He prayed for the wicked men who cried out for His death—*"Father, FORGIVE THEM, for they know not what they do!"* (Luke 23:34).

Christ suffered at the hands of the devil:—

"Then was Jesus led up of the Spirit into the wilderness to be tempted of the devil. And when He had fasted forty days and forty nights, He was afterward an hungred. And when the tempter came to Him, he said, If thou be the Son of God, command that these stones be made bread. But He answered and said, It is written, Man shall not live by bread alone, but by every word that proceedeth out of the mouth of God.

"Then the devil taketh Him up into the holy city, and setteth Him on a pinnacle of the temple, and saith unto Him, If thou be the Son of God, cast thyself down: for it is written, He shall give His angels charge concerning thee: and in their hands they shall bear thee up, lest at any time thou dash thy foot against a stone. Jesus said unto him, It is written again, Thou shalt not tempt the Lord thy God.

"Again, the devil taketh Him up into an exceeding high mountain, and sheweth Him all the kingdoms of the world, and the glory of them; and saith unto Him, All these things will I give thee, if thou wilt fall down and worship me. Then saith Jesus unto him, Get thee hence, Satan: for it is written, Thou shalt worship the Lord thy God, and Him only shalt thou serve.

"Then the devil leaveth Him, and behold, ANGELS CAME AND MINISTERED UNTO HIM" (Matt. 4: 1—11).

Jesus was tempted in all points as we are tempted, yet without sin (Heb. 4:15). Satan the cunning one, the deceiver, brought all of his power into use against the Lamb of God—with one purpose in mind: *to keep Jesus from going to the cross and dying in our place!* If he could have kept the Son of God from Calvary he could have damned every soul to the lake of fire. Failing with the temptation in the wilderness, he retreated to make new plans and attack again.

In the Garden of Gethsemane the devil marshalled all of the forces of hell against the praying Saviour. I believe Psalm 22 bears this out. In verses 12 and 13 of that Psalm we read, "Many bulls have compassed me: strong bulls of Bashan have beset me round. They gaped upon me with their mouths, as a ravening and a roaring lion." Demon-dogs, bulls of Bashan—all of the demon monstrosities of hell attacked Jesus in the Garden of Gethsemane, and His sweat became as great drops of blood falling to the ground (Luke 22: 39—44). Mankind will never know such agony as the Lamb of God endured in the Garden as Satan attempted once again to frustrate God's plan and keep Christ from reaching Calvary.

But hallelujah! In spite of all that the devil and his cohorts could devise and carry out, the only begotten Son of God, the Sacrificial Lamb, marched on to the cross! He conquered the world, the flesh, and the devil, death, hell, and the grave—and *we are MORE than conquerors through Him* (Rom. 8:37).

70

Past: The Crucifixion

The greatest suffering of all:—

The greatest suffering through which Christ passed was the suffering He endured from God the Father. It is true that wicked men tried and *convicted* Jesus and sentenced Him to death. It is true that He was *crucified* by the hands of wicked men. But man did not and could not put Him to death! His life could never have been taken had He not been *"smitten of God"* (Isa. 53:4).

The Apostle Paul tells us that God "spared not His own Son, but *delivered Him up for us all"* (Rom. 8:32). God delivered His Son into the hands of wicked men— why? *"For us ALL!"* God laid our sin on His Son and condemned Him for our sake. His death was not according to nature, nor was it by the hand of man. His death was from above, by the hand of Almighty God: "It pleased the Lord to bruise Him; He hath put Him to grief." It was God who "hath made His soul an offering for sin," God "hath poured out His soul unto death" (Isa. 53:10—12). God made Jesus to be sin for us; and since God cannot look upon sin *He had to forsake Jesus in order to accept US.*

Therefore from the darkness which enshrouded Calvary came the agonizing cry, *"My God! My God! Why hast thou forsaken me?"* Here was made known the awful, indescribable suffering of the Lamb of God, the Substitute for sinners—yes, for you and for me. Such agony and suffering Jesus endured from the hand of a holy God in order that God might be just and yet justify sinners through the shed blood of His only begotten Son. *"Surely He hath borne OUR griefs, and carried OUR sorrows: yet we did esteem Him stricken, smitten of God, and afflicted. . . . He was wounded for OUR transgressions, He was bruised for OUR iniquities: the chastisement of OUR peace was*

71

upon Him; and with HIS stripes WE are healed" (Isa. 53:4, 5).

The hour of Christ's greatest agony, knowing that God had forsaken Him, was the hour when the great work of atonement was accomplished—once, for all, forever. God's hand rested on His only begotten Son *as He laid on HIM* "the iniquity of us all" (Isa. 53:6).

Elsewhere in the Old Testament Scriptures we read references to the same atoning work of the Lamb of God when He took the sinner's place:

"All thy waves and thy billows are gone over me" (Psalm 42:7).

"Thine arrows stick fast in me and thine hand presseth me sore" (Psalm 38:2).

"Thou hast laid me in the lowest pit, in darkness, in the deeps. Thy wrath lieth hard upon me, and thou hast afflicted me with all thy waves" (Psalm 88:6, 7).

". . . I suffer thy terrors . . . Thy fierce wrath goeth over me" (Psalm 88:15, 16).

Never—no, *never*—shall the finite mind of man fully discover or understand the greatness of the price Jesus paid that we might be saved. Never will we be able to comprehend the sorrow, affliction, terror, and fierce wrath that rested upon Him because of our sin.

"It Is Finished!"

"When Jesus therefore had received the vinegar, He said, IT IS FINISHED! And He bowed His head, and gave up the ghost" (John 19:30).

Christ's work on the cross is singular. It stands alone. No other event in heaven or on earth compares with the death of the Lamb of God on Calvary. It can never be repeated—and because of its *eternal efficacy* it will never *need* to be repeated.

"It is finished!" (The Greek reads, "It is *accom-*

plished.")   This was His cry of victory on the cross. The great work He came to do—to take away the sin of the world and purchase redemption for us—is finished.   Nothing can be added, there is nothing man can *do, say, live,* or *be* that will add to the finished work of the Lord Jesus Christ.   He *left nothing undone,* and *by faith we appropriate all that He did.* In the temple, the veil hangs rent in twain from top to bottom—mute testimony to His statement "It is finished."   The open tomb testifies to the same.

What has been *accomplished* in this blessed finished work of the Lamb of God? We cannot grasp the full meaning of His accomplishment now, we cannot fathom the depths of His finished work. "Now we see through a glass, *darkly*" (I Cor. 13:12); but one day when we sit in the heavenly Bible class, the Lord Himself will explain to us all that He accomplished *for* us that we could never have accomplished for ourselves. When we are transformed into His own image, when we become like Him (I John 3:2), when we shall have shared with Him in His glorious inheritance (Rom. 8:17), then shall we know more fully what Christ accomplished for us at Calvary.

"The last enemy that shall be destroyed is death" (I Cor. 15:26); and when death and sin are no more, the redeemed shall dwell in that Pearly White City and gaze down upon this earth created anew. *Then* we shall fully know that all that we *have,* all that we *are,* all that we ever *hope to have or be* has its source in the finished work of Christ at Calvary. The Gospel preached to lost, guilty sinners is based upon the eternal, divine fact that Christ died for all, for *whosoever* will come to Him in faith believing.

John the Beloved declares, "My little children, these things write I unto you, that ye sin not. And if any

73

man sin, we have an Advocate with the Father, Jesus Christ the righteous: and He is the propitiation for our sins—and not for *our's only,* but also *for the sins of the whole world"* (I John 2:1,2). Every believer, looking back to the cross, can say: *"God loved me* and gave His only begotten Son to die for me. *Christ* loved me and gave Himself for me. He paid my debt, He took my place. He bore my sins in His own body on the cross. He satisfied God's holiness, God's righteousness, *for me.* He was *my Substitute.* He tasted death for me that I might not die."

There is much error being taught in this present day. There are men who teach universal salvation, larger hope, Millennial nomism, and many other "isms." Such teachings emanate from the fact that men do not correctly understand the difference between *propitiation* and *substitution.* Propitiation is the *God-ward* side of the sacrifice of the Lamb of God, the sacrifice by which God's holiness and righteousness are satisfied. Christ's propitiation is for the whole wide world, but this does not mean that the whole world will be *saved.* Certainly some people will *not* be saved, because they refuse to hear the Gospel and believe in *the finished work* of Jesus. He *loves* the whole world, He *died* for the whole world, and He is *the SUBSTITUTE* for all who will *believe* on His precious name. In other words, the ransom is paid for every sinner who has ever been born or ever will be born—but there will always be some who choose not to *accept* what Christ did for them. They prefer to go on in sin, they refuse to be delivered from the wages of sin—death in the lake that burns with fire and brimstone, *eternal damnation.* God does not *send* men to hell! They go there because they refuse to believe on His only begotten Son, the Lord Jesus

Christ. God's Word plainly declares, "He that *believeth* on Him is *not condemned:* but he that believeth *not* is condemned *already,* because he hath not believed in the name of the only begotten Son of God" (John 3:18).

Our Possession In Christ

What do believers possess now? We could give many, many Scriptures which relate to our present possessions in Christ, but time and space will not permit us to give them all. So we will look at just a few of them.

Sons of God:—

First of all, we are *sons of God* now. We are not *"going to be"* sons of God when we die or when Jesus comes. We are sons of God NOW, this very moment, in this present world:

"Behold, what manner of love the Father hath bestowed upon us, that we should be called *the sons of God.* Therefore the world knoweth us not, because it knew Him not. Beloved, *NOW are we the sons of God,* and it doth not yet appear what we *shall be:* but we know that, when He shall appear, we shall be like Him; for we shall see Him as He is" (I John 3: 1, 2).

Possessors of the Holy Spirit:—

As sons of God in this present world, we also possess the *Holy Spirit* now. God's infallible Word declares it:

". . . Now if any man *have not* the Spirit of Christ, he is none of His. . . . For as many as are led by the Spirit of God, they are the sons of God. . . . The Spirit Himself beareth witness with our spirit, that we *are* the children of God" (Rom. 8:9, 14, 16).

The fulness of the Godhead:—

In Christ we possess *the fulness of the Godhead,* "for IN HIM dwelleth all the fulness of the Godhead bodily. And ye are *complete in Him,* which is the head of all principality and power" (Col. 2:9, 10).

Justification:—

In Christ we possess *perfect justification.* The Lamb of God "was delivered for our offences, and was raised again for our justification" (Rom. 4:25). Since *Christ is perfect,* He provides only perfect justification. Our sins are forever put away because He bore them on the cross and paid for them by His sacrificial death. The blood of Jesus not only delivers from the *penalty* of sin, but also cleanses us *progressively* from all sin:

"If we walk in the light, as HE is in the light, we have fellowship one with another, *and the blood of Jesus Christ His Son cleanseth us from ALL sin*" (I John 1:7). Therefore I ask with the Apostle Paul:

"What shall we then say to these things? If God be for us, who can be against us? He that spared not His own Son, but delivered Him up for us all, how shall He not with Him also freely give us all things? Who shall lay anything to the charge of God's elect? It is God that *justifieth.* Who is he that condemneth? *It is Christ that died,* yea rather, that is risen again, who is even at the right hand of God, who also maketh intercession for us.

"Who shall separate us from the love of Christ? Shall tribulation, or distress, or persecution, or famine, or nakedness, or peril, or sword? As it is written, For thy sake we are killed all the day long; we are accounted as sheep for the slaughter.

"Nay, in all these things we are *more than conquerors* through Him that loved us. *For I am persuaded, that neither death, nor life, nor angels, nor principalities, nor powers, nor things present, nor things to come, nor height, nor depth, NOR ANY OTHER CREATURE, shall be able to separate us from the love of God, which is in Christ Jesus our Lord"* (Rom. 8:31—39).

Peace with God:—

In Christ we possess *perfect peace*—peace "which passeth all understanding" (Phil. 4:7). We possess *peace with God* because Christ "made peace through the blood of His cross, by Him to reconcile all things unto Himself; by Him, I say, whether they be things in earth, or things in heaven" (Col. 1:20). Jesus said to His disciples, "Peace I leave with you, *MY peace* I give unto you: not as the world giveth, give I unto you. Let not your heart be troubled, neither let it be afraid" (John 14:27).

Christ IS our peace: "Therefore being justified by faith, we have peace *with* God through our Lord Jesus Christ, by whom also we have access by faith into this grace wherein we stand, and rejoice in hope of the glory of God" (Rom. 5:1, 2). Many believers think that their peace *with* God depends on their walk, their work, their daily living; and if they sin they fear they have lost their peace and their standing before God, needing to be restored in their hearts lest they be lost forever. Nothing could be further from the truth! I am so glad our God loves us with perfect love, a love unlike our love for our fellowman. It is not our walk, our service, or anything we say or do that sets the foundation for peace with God. On the contrary, our peace *with* God rests entirely on what God has done for us in Christ's finished work on the cross.

It is true that our walk and our service, what we do or do not do, will determine our reward for stewardship; but there is a difference between stewardship and justification—or *redemption.* In I Corinthians 3:11—15 we read, "Other foundation can no man lay than that is laid, which is Jesus Christ. Now if any man build upon this foundation gold, silver, precious stones, wood, hay, stubble; every man's work shall be made manifest: for the day shall declare it, because it shall be revealed by fire; and *the fire shall try every man's work of what SORT it is.* If any man's work abide which he hath built thereupon, *he shall receive a reward. If any man's WORK shall be burned, he shall suffer loss"* (loss of reward) *"but HE HIMSELF SHALL BE SAVED; yet so as by fire."* Our peace *with* God, perfect peace, depends upon the perfect sacrifice made for us by the Lord Jesus Christ, God's only begotten Son.

Acceptance before God:—

In Christ we have *perfect standing before God,* perfect *acceptance* with Him and *perfect access* to Him. Believers are made nigh unto God by the blood of the Lamb (Eph. 2:13). We are *"accepted in the Beloved"* (Eph. 1:6). The believer can stand in God's presence— cleansed, sanctified, complete in Christ, as near to God as Christ is near to Him because we are "hid with Christ in God" (Col. 3:3). We are dead to the world, dead to sin, dead to the law, and dead to self. The "old man" is crucified with Christ, and sin shall not have dominion over us:

"Knowing this, that *our old man is crucified with Him,* that the body of sin might be destroyed, that henceforth we should not serve sin, for *he that is*

78

DEAD is FREED FROM SIN. Now if we be dead
with Christ, we believe that we shall also live with
Him: knowing that Christ being raised from the dead
dieth no more; death hath no more dominion over Him.
For in that He died, He died unto sin once: but in
that He liveth, He liveth unto God. *Likewise reckon
ye also yourselves to be dead indeed unto sin, but
alive unto God THROUGH JESUS CHRIST OUR
LORD"* (Rom. 6:6—11).

The Apostle Paul declares, "They that are Christ's
have crucified the flesh with the affections and lusts"
(Gal. 5:24), and in Galatians 2:20 he gives this personal
testimony: "I am crucified with Christ: nevertheless I
live; yet not I, but Christ liveth in me: and the life
which I now live in the flesh I live *by the faith of the
Son of God,* who loved me and gave Himself for me."

Deliverance from the power of darkness:—

In Christ, believers have deliverance from the darkness of sin and from the *power* of darkness. This is
the assurance given so plainly in God's Word. God has
"delivered us from the power of darkness, and hath
translated us into the kingdom of His dear Son: in
whom we have *redemption THROUGH HIS BLOOD,*
even the forgiveness of sins" (Col. 1:13, 14).

Paul declares, "Ye were sometimes *darkness,* but
NOW are ye light in the Lord: walk as children of
light" (Eph. 5:8). In I Thessalonians 5:5 Paul tells
us, "Ye are all the children of light, and the children
of the day: *we are not of the night, nor of DARK-
NESS."* Then in I Peter 2:9 we read, "Ye are a chosen generation, a royal priesthood, an holy nation, a
peculiar people; that ye should shew forth the praises
of Him who hath called you *out of DARKNESS into
His marvellous light!"*

A perfect inheritance:—

In Christ, believers possess the title to an eternal in-heritance. God has "begotten us again unto a lively hope *by the resurrection of Jesus Christ from the dead, to an INHERITANCE incorruptible, and undefiled, and that fadeth not away,* reserved in heaven for you" (I Pet. 1:3, 4). Therefore, according to God's Word, we have *a perfect inheritance,* reserved in heaven for us.

"Blessed assurance! Jesus is mine. Oh, what a fore-taste of glory divine!" There is no uncertainty attached to the hope of a born again believer. We have salva-tion, we are saved *forever.* We have eternal life. We are sons of God—yes, even in this present evil world we are children of the heavenly King, heirs of God and joint-heirs with Christ. We are led by the Holy Spirit, sealed by the Holy Spirit until the day of redemption; and beyond this life we have an inheritance eternal and undefiled, reserved in heaven for us.

To this can be added the divine truth that *on the cross* Jesus loved *individuals,* He loved *the Church* made up of individual believers, and He loved and died for *Israel.* In I Corinthians 10:32 we are com-manded, "Give none offence, neither to the *Jews,* nor to the *Gentiles,* nor to the *Church of God"—*the Church purchased with His own blood (Acts 20:28).

Christ loved the world—He gave His life "that who-soever believeth in Him should not perish, but have everlasting life" (John 3:16). He loved the Church, His bride, "and gave Himself for it; that He might sanctify and cleanse it with the washing of water by the Word, that He might present it to Himself a glorious Church, not having spot, or wrinkle, or any such thing; but that it should be holy and without blemish" (Eph. 5: 25—27). He loved Israel, He died for the Jews as well as for each individual and for the Church; and one day the nation Israel will own Him as Messiah: "In that day there shall be a fountain opened to the house of David and to the inhabitants of Jerusalem for sin and uncleanness. . . . And one shall say unto Him, What are these wounds in thine hands?   Then He shall answer, Those with which I was wounded in the house of my friends" (Zech. 13:1, 6).

All deliverance points to Calvary.   All things in heaven and in earth will be reconciled in virtue of the death of Jesus on the cross.   One day all suffering will cease, all creation will be delivered from the curse. In Romans 8:18—23 Paul testifies:

"I reckon that the sufferings of this present time are not worthy to be compared with the glory which shall be revealed in us.   For the earnest expectation of the creature waiteth for the manifestation of the sons of God.   For the creature was made subject to vanity, not willingly, but by reason of Him who hath subjected the same in hope.   Because the creature itself also shall be *delivered from the bondage of corruption into the glorious liberty of the children of God.   FOR WE KNOW THAT THE WHOLE CREATION GROANETH AND TRAVAILETH IN PAIN TOGETHER UNTIL NOW.* And not only they, but ourselves also, which have the firstfruits of the Spirit, even we ourselves groan within ourselves, *waiting for the adoption—to wit, THE REDEMPTION OF OUR BODY!"*

Thus by His finished work on the cross, the Lord Jesus Christ will deliver the whole creation from the curse, and will create all things new.

Ye Are Not Your Own

"What?   Know ye not that your body is the temple of the Holy Ghost which is in you, which ye have of God, and *ye are not your own? For YE ARE BOUGHT*

WITH A PRICE: therefore glorify God in your body, and in your spirit, which are God's" (I Cor. 6:19, 20).

God loved us so much that He gave His only begotten Son to suffer horrible agony and cruel death on the cross of Calvary that we might be saved. Jesus loved us so much that He took our sins and bore them in His own body on the cross, nailing them there.

Therefore, *positionally*, believers are *dead* through the death of Jesus. We have died to the old life, to the law, to the world. Beloved, *this very moment* we are walking, talking, living as dead to sin and alive unto God. A child of God who walks after the flesh thereby denies the power and the value of the blessed work of Christ at Calvary. He cried out, "It is finished!" but Christians who live defeated lives testify "It is *NOT finished.*" Regardless of how we live, however, *it IS finished,* and if we are not enjoying our spiritual birthright we have no one to blame but ourselves. We are more than conquerors through Christ, and He has made provision for any and every temptation that comes our way. God's Word emphatically declares that no temptation comes to us *"but such as is common to man."* It further declares, *"GOD IS FAITHFUL, who will not suffer you to be tempted above that ye are able;* but will with the temptation also make a way to escape, that ye may be able to bear it!" (I Cor. 10:13). Then the Apostle Paul gives his own personal testimony—which we, too, can experience: *"I can do all things THROUGH CHRIST which strengtheneth me. . . . God forbid that I should glory, save in the cross of our Lord Jesus Christ, by whom the world is crucified unto me, and I unto the world"* (Phil. 4:13; Gal. 6:14).

God grant that we, too, may exalt the cross of Christ in our lives.

Chapter II

THE PRESENT WORK OF CHRIST

"God, who at sundry times and in divers manners spake in time past unto the fathers by the prophets, hath in these last days spoken unto us by His Son, whom He hath appointed heir of all things, by whom also He made the worlds; who being the brightness of His glory, and the express image of His Person, and upholding all things by the Word of His power, when He had by Himself purged our sins, sat down on the right hand of the Majesty on high" (Heb. 1:1–3).

The only begotten Son of God came into the world to put away sin by the sacrifice of Himself, and His finished work on the cross is the basis for His *present* and *future* work. Through His death on the cross He procured redemption for us; and in His present and future work He brings this great redemption into eternal results.

There is much confusion among Christians concerning the present and the future work of the Lord Jesus Christ. Some people speak of Him even now as King of kings and Lord of lords, reigning over the earth. They pray, "Thy kingdom come," not knowing for what they pray. To them, the Church is the kingdom; and that kingdom, gradually being enlarged under the spiritual reign of Christ, will continue to be enlarged until the whole world has been *brought into* the kingdom. So—they pray for souls to be added to the Church in order to bring in the kingdom!

This is error. The Church was not put here on earth to bring in the kingdom, but *to call out a people for the name of Jesus,* through the preaching of the Gospel of the grace of God. I know no passage in all of the Word of God that so clearly states the mission of the Church in this Dispensation of Grace (and immediately afterward) as Acts 15:13—18 when the Apostle James spoke at the council in Jerusalem:

"After they had held their peace, James answered, saying, Men and brethren, hearken unto me: Simeon hath declared how God at the first did visit the Gentiles, to take out of them a people for His name. And to this agree the words of the prophets; as it is written, After this I will return, and will build again the tabernacle of David, which is fallen down; and I will build again the ruins thereof, and I will set it up: that the residue of men might seek after the Lord, and all the Gentiles, upon whom my name is called, saith the Lord, who doeth all these things. Known unto God are all His works from the beginning of the world."

The Church is not the kingdom, the Church is the body of Christ. Therefore to teach that the Church will bring in the kingdom is wrongly dividing the Word of truth. It is true that Christ will have a kingdom of glory and righteousness, a kingdom of peace, and He will reign over the earth. There *will be* "peace on earth, good will toward men"—but not until the Prince of Peace shall come and put Satan in the pit. As long as the devil is out of the lake of fire there will be no lasting peace, and there will continue to be a scarcity of good will among men. Only when Jesus descends from heaven to chain and bind Lucifer, put him into hell and set a seal on him, will there be peace on earth and good will among men. Satan will be sealed in the pit for a thousand years, and during that time men will beat their swords into plowshares and their spears into pruning hooks. They will study war no more, and there will be one thousand years of the glorious reign of King Jesus as He sits on the throne of David and reigns from Jerusalem. There *will be* a righteous government on earth; but—I repeat —only when Jesus *visibly returns* to earth and His feet stand on the Mount of Olives (Zech. 14:4). His rule as King of kings is in the future. His present work is of an entirely different nature.

What Is the Present Work of Christ?

"There is one God, and one Mediator between God and men, the Man Christ Jesus; who gave Himself a ransom for all, to be testified in due time" (I Tim. 2:5, 6).

On the cross our blessed Lord gave the body God had prepared for Him, the body He had taken in the Incarnation. That body died—it was the only part of Christ that *could* die. *God* cannot die, and Christ was God in flesh. His body of flesh was dishonored by man—scourged, buffeted, spit upon, nailed to a cross—but it did not see *corruption,* for Christ rose from the dead just as prophecy declared He would (Psalm 16:10), and as Jesus Himself declared He would rise again the third day (John 2:19).

It was not possible that death should hold the Lamb of God. The mighty power of God opened the grave and raised Him from the dead; and this same mighty power of God is the power which is toward us who believe (Eph. 1:19). God not only raised Jesus from the dead, He also *"gave Him glory,* that (our) faith

85

and hope might be in God" (I Pet. 1:21).

The greatest bombshell ever to explode in the face of an unbelieving world was the bodily resurrection of the Lord Jesus Christ. That He rose physically, bodily, is an indisputable fact attested to by many witnesses. To the Corinthian believers Paul restated *the Gospel,* which is the death, burial, and resurrection of Jesus "according to the Scriptures." He then gave testimony that the risen Christ "was seen of *Cephas,* then of the *twelve:* after that, He was seen of *above five hundred brethren at once* . . . After that, He was seen of *James,* then of *all the apostles."* Then Paul adds, "And last of all He was seen *of me also,* as of one born out of due time" (I Cor. 15:1−8).

If Christ did *not* rise bodily from the grave, then there IS no resurrection. If Christ had not risen, His death on the cross would have no more meaning than the death of any other martyr, any other mortal man. If He had not risen, then His blood shed on the cross could never take away our sins, nor give rest to the guilty conscience, nor redeem lost sinners. In addition to that, if Christ had not risen from the dead, then all who have passed from this life, having placed their trust in Him, would be perished. Paul expressed these truths in I Corinthians 15:12−20:

"Now if Christ be preached that He rose from the dead, how say some among you that there is no resurrection of the dead? But if there be no resurrection of the dead, then is Christ not risen: and if Christ be not risen, then is our preaching vain, and your faith is also vain. Yea, and we are found false witnesses of God; because we have testified of God that He raised up Christ: whom He raised not up, if so be that the dead rise not. For if the dead rise not, then is not Christ raised: and if Christ be not raised,

86

your faith is vain; ye are yet in your sins. Then they also which are fallen asleep in Christ are perished. If in this life only we have hope in Christ, we are of all men most miserable!" And then hear his shout of faith victorious: *"BUT NOW IS CHRIST RISEN FROM THE DEAD, and become the firstfruits of them that slept!"*

There can be no doubt that Christ's resurrection was physical, and all one need do to believe in His bodily resurrection is to simply accept the Word of God. To *deny* the bodily resurrection of Jesus is to deny *the Word of God.* The disciples in the upper room not only *saw and recognized* the risen Lord, they were also invited to touch Him and prove to themselves that He was flesh and bone, not a spirit. Then to further prove His physical resurrection Jesus asked for meat, they gave Him broiled fish and honeycomb, and He *ate* in their presence. Anyone who will accept the Word of God will readily accept the fact of the bodily resurrection of Jesus.

Christ, "in the days of His flesh . . . offered up prayers and supplications with strong crying and tears unto Him that was able to save Him from death . . ." (Heb. 5:7). (The Greek reads *"OUT of death."*) Yes, Jesus rose again physically. His resurrection from the dead was God's answer to the prayer He prayed with strong crying and tears. His bodily resurrection was God's "Amen!" to His finished work.

By raising Jesus from the dead, God the Father set His seal of approval on the work of His Son on the cross and on everything He said and did in His earthly ministry. *Now* guilty, ungodly men can be righteously acquitted of guilt, because God's eternal righteousness and holiness were upheld and satisfied by Christ's payment of the full penalty for sin.

87

Even before God sent a messenger from heaven to roll away the stone from the door of the tomb where Christ's body lay, He had shown that the work of His Son was altogether satisfactory and pleasing to Him. When Jesus cried from the cross, "It is finished!" the heavenly Father reached down with His mighty hand and split the veil in the temple from top to bottom. No hand of man could have rent that impenetrable veil which hid the holy of holies from the eyes of men. It was torn by the hand of Almighty God, thus opening the way into the holy of holies for all who will come through the veil of Christ's flesh—His riven side. A holy and righteous God can now come forth in fullest blessing to man, *sinful man,* bought by such a price! Through the precious blood of Jesus man can approach the presence of God and be at home with Him—a loving Father who gave His only *begotten* Son that we might become sons, heirs of God and joint-heirs with Christ.

Now, in this Dispensation of Grace, sinners saved by the grace of God are invited to enter boldly "into the holiest by the blood of Jesus, by a new and living way, which He hath consecrated for us, through the veil, that is to say, His flesh" (Heb. 10:19, 20).

Lest there be some misunderstanding about the body in which Christ came forth from the grave, we have already declared the truth of the Scriptures—namely, that He arose with the body He had taken in the Incarnation. He left the grave in corporeal form, a tangible body that could be seen and touched. The nail prints in His hands and feet were still visible. The scar from the Roman spear could still be seen in His side. When He appears to Israel (Zech. 13:6, 7) those same scars will still be visible. But I would also point out that while Christ rose from the grave in the same body He was given in the Incarnation, His resurrection body was a *glorified* body—and such will *we* be in the first resurrection. *He will "change our vile body, that it may be fashioned like unto His glorious body,* according to the working whereby He is able even to subdue all things unto Himself" (Phil. 3:21).

Believers are still waiting for the redemption of the body (Rom. 8:23). Those who sleep in Jesus also wait for the shout, the voice of the archangel and the trumpet of God, that will call us to meet Christ in the air (I Thess. 4:16—18). The dead in Christ will then be raised incorruptible and living believers will be changed—"in a moment, in the twinkling of an eye" (I Cor. 15:51,52), and together we will be caught up to meet Jesus; *and so shall we ever be with the Lord!*

The Apostle Paul explains that the natural body "is sown in *corruption,* it is raised in *incorruption.* It is sown in *dishonour;* it is raised in *glory;* it is sown in *weakness,* it is raised in *power.* It is sown a *natural* body; it is raised a *spiritual* body. . . . And so it is written, the *first* man *Adam* was made a living soul; the *last Adam* (Christ) was made *a quickening spirit"* (I Cor. 15:42—45).

It was Jesus *in His tangible, resurrection body* who ascended into heaven while the astonished disciples gazed after Him in amazement. He had taken them out from Jerusalem to the Mount of Olives, and in His last moments with them He instructed them to wait for Pentecost, after which, endued with power from on high, they should take up the work He was leaving in their hands and should be witnesses for Him—first in Jerusalem, then in all Judaea and in Samaria, and finally unto the uttermost parts of the earth. "And when He had spoken these things, *while*

89

they beheld, He was taken up; and a cloud received Him out of their sight.

"And while they looked stedfastly toward heaven as He went up, behold, two men stood by them in white apparel; which also said, *Ye men of Galilee, why stand ye gazing up into heaven? THIS SAME JESUS, which is taken up from you into heaven, SHALL SO COME IN LIKE MANNER AS YE HAVE SEEN HIM GO INTO HEAVEN"* (Acts 1:9—11).

I believe the Psalmist was speaking of the ascension of Christ when he wrote, *"God is gone up with a shout, the Lord with the sound of a trumpet"* (Psalm 47:5). What a glorious, triumphant entrance into heaven—with a shout and the sound of a trumpet! Shekinah glory received the Son of God and enveloped Him as He ascended where the physical eye could not follow Him. Now He sits at the Father's right hand with all of the glory and honor He possessed with the Father from eternity, and one day *that same Jesus* will come again, just as He went away—with the archangel, with the trump of God, with the Victor's shout! and when He comes, He will be attended by mighty angels. He will descend into the atmospheric heavens and will call believers up to meet Him in the air. Then when He comes in the *second phase* of His second coming (in the Revelation), every eye shall see Him and all the kindreds of the earth shall wail because of Him (Rev. 1:7). Thus will it be "when the Son of man shall come *in His glory, and all the holy angels with Him"* (Matt. 25:31).

When Jesus ascended back to the Father, *Satan had to step aside* because the risen Lord passed directly through Satan's territory! Ephesians 2:2 tells us that the devil is "the prince of the power of the air." The atmospheric heavens are literally filled with demons and evil spirits, emissaries of the devil; but when the Son of God ascended back to heaven the evil forces had to stand back in fear and trembling as the glorified Christ passed on higher and higher until He reached the third heaven, the Father's house, and sat down at the right hand of God.

God welcomed His Son home: "Wherefore God also hath highly exalted Him, and given Him a name which is above every name: that at the name of Jesus every knee should bow, of things in heaven, and things in earth, and things under the earth; and that every tongue should confess that Jesus Christ is Lord, to the glory of God the Father" (Phil. 2:9—11).

Thank God, there is a MAN in heaven now—a Man in a real body of flesh and bones, a Man who was tempted in all points as we are tempted—yet without sin. He is seated at the right hand of God, making intercession for us. I cannot over-emphasize the fact that the Lord Jesus Christ is *corporeally present* at this moment in the highest heaven, seated with God in the highest seat in heaven, and everything we have or hope to have in the spiritual life depends upon this truth. If Christ's physical resurrection were not truth, then His past work would have no meaning, His present work would be non-existent, and His future work would be an utter impossibility! To deny that Jesus rose bodily and is at this moment seated at the right hand of God is to rob ourselves of every promise, every comfort, every joy, and the peace that dwells in the heart of believers.

I fully realize that there are cults and sects today where teachers and preachers *deny* the bodily resurrection of Jesus. These false teachers also deny the *deity* of Jesus. To deny either His deity or His bodily resurrection is to also deny His bodily presence in heaven at this moment. This, of course, denies the authority of the Word of God—and such denial would destroy the foundation of Christianity. There are too many cults, too many false religions, to take up time and space to name and discuss them here; but their teachings are actually not new, for even in the days when John the Beloved penned his epistles under inspiration of the Holy Spirit there were such men in the world—and they have been here ever since!

II John 7 tells us, "Many deceivers are entered into the world, who confess not that Jesus Christ is come in the flesh. This is a deceiver and an antichrist."

The Apostle Paul also warns against false teachers. In II Corinthians 11:13—15 he says, "Such are false apostles, deceitful workers, transforming themselves into the apostles of Christ. And no marvel—for Satan himself is transformed into an angel of light. Therefore it is no great thing if his ministers also be transformed as the ministers of righteousness, whose end shall be according to their works."

Peter warns, "Be sober, be vigilant; because your adversary the devil, as a roaring lion, walketh about, seeking whom he may devour" (I Pet. 5:8).

Satan has an abundance of disguises. He can come as a roaring lion—more than likely he will come as an angel of light. His ministers, many of whom stand in the pulpits of America today, are so well disguised as ministers of righteousness that the discernment of the Holy Spirit is required to differentiate between them. How does the Christian tell the true from the false? The answer is found in the Word of God. In I Peter 2:6 the Word declares, "Wherefore also it is contained in the Scripture, Behold, I lay in Sion a chief corner stone, elect, precious: *and he that be-lieveth on Him SHALL NOT BE CONFOUNDED*"—

or *confused.*

Beloved, if you are born again you have the Person of the Holy Spirit dwelling in your heart. The "Stone" of this Scripture is Christ, and if Christ is dwelling in your heart, He will not allow you to be confounded or confused about false teachers. *"Ye have an unction from the Holy One,* and ye know all things. . . . *The anointing which ye have received of Him abideth in you,* and ye need not that any man teach you: but as the same anointing teacheth you of all things, and is truth, and is no lie, and even as it hath taught you, ye shall abide in Him"* (I John 2:20, 27).

The Holy Spirit in the heart of the believer warns against error and reveals truth. Therefore if you do not know the difference between truth and error, my advice to you is to be born again. Seek Bible salvation, and you will be able to distinguish between false teachers and the ministers of God.

It is in His resurrection body that the Man Christ Jesus sits at the right hand of God from whence He carries on His present work on our behalf.

As our Mediator:—

The Scripture plainly declares that there is but ONE Mediator between God and man—"the Man Christ Jesus" (I Tim. 2:5). No other one could span the great gulf between a holy God and sinful humanity. Job 9:33 expresses it in these words: *"Neither is there any daysman betwixt us, that might lay his hand upon us both."* The figure set forth here is of a man who, in order to reconcile an argument, stands between two men who have had a disagreement and lays his hand on each of them. In the Lord Jesus Christ God has provided a divine Daysman to stand between poor sinful man and a holy God. Jesus, in

His twofold nature, is in a position to "lay His hand on us both"—i. e., He is the hand of Deity because He is God; He is the hand of humanity because He is "the Man, Christ Jesus." Thus He lays upon us the hand of Divinity and the hand of humanity—both hands bearing the scars which testify to the tremendous cost of our redemption. Those scars are the seal of the mediation between sinful man and Jehovah God, perfected through the death of Jesus, the price of our ransom—*demanded* by God's holiness, *paid for* by God's love, *provided for all* and *presented on behalf of all*, whether they accept it or not!

In the Garden of Eden, Adam sinned and broke communion with God. God was offended, Adam was the offender. But Jesus (the last Adam) was God the offended One, in the flesh that offended Him. In Jesus we have both the Offended and the offender. Thus there is only one Mediator between God and man, and the only possible way man can ever stand before God's holiness is IN Christ Jesus. IN HIM we are holy and righteous. Apart from Him we are hopelessly lost. Our Mediator then is not an angel, not our pastor, not an evangelist, not a bishop, not the pope, not a priest, not the Virgin Mary—but the Man Christ Jesus. And if we ever stand before God to hear Him say, "Well done," it will be because Jesus is our Mediator and Confessor before God the Father (Matt. 10:32), and He will exercise His office of Mediator throughout this Dispensation of Grace, on behalf of all who by personal faith have accepted Him as Saviour and Lord.

As our Advocate:—

"My little children, these things write I unto you, that ye sin not. And if any man sin, we have an

Advocate with the Father, Jesus Christ the righteous:
and He is the propitiation for our sins: and not for
our's only, but also for the sins of the whole world"
(I John 2:1, 2).

Some believers think that Christ's priesthood and
His advocacy are one and the same, but this is not
true. His advocacy is that which restores us after we
have sinned. God does not want His little children
to sin, and you can rest assured that sin breaks fellowship between the Christian and God. But believers
do sin sometimes, and "if we say that we have not
sinned, we make God a liar, and His Word is not
in us" (I John 1:10). I repeat—God does not want us
to sin; but if His child sins "we have an Advocate
with the Father"—and without our Advocate we could
never find forgiveness for sins committed after we are
born again.

The first chapter of I John makes known our wonderful privilege as believers, and in verse 4 we read,
"These things write we unto you, *that your JOY may
be full.*" We are to be in fellowship with the Father,
and we fellowship with the Father when we delight
ourselves in His blessed Son. In fact, the only way
in which we *can* fellowship with God is through His
Son in whom He delights. When we share the Father's own thoughts about Christ, we fellowship with
God the Father and with God the Son.

Christ knoweth the Father, He has revealed Him
to us, and has brought us *into His own relationship*
with the Father. Fellowship with Christ is the enjoyment of this relationship with God, and the condition of the enjoyment of this privilege is that we
walk in the light as HE is in the light: "If we walk
in the light as He is in the light, we have fellowship
one with another, and the blood of Jesus Christ His

95

Son cleanseth us from all sin" (I John 1:7).

Thank God, sin cannot rob the born again believer of salvation, but sin *in the LIFE of a believer* robs him of joy, fellowship, and reward. The Bible standard is, *"Child of God, SIN NOT!"* We should live in constant fellowship with God the Father and God the Son. This is the fellowship which grace has brought us, the position in which grace has placed us, and if we abide there continually we do not sin— but how often we come short of walking as we *should* walk, in grace and in fellowship with God! When we fail to walk as we should, we fall into sin, and whether it be a sin of *omission* or a sin of *commission,* the Christian *knows* when he sins. It is then that we turn to our Advocate, Jesus Christ the Righteous One *who never sinned.*

I am so glad that God's Word does not say, "We have an Advocate with the Father if we straighten up our life, if we change our mind, etc." The intercession of our Advocate on our behalf is independent of our doing, just as our *salvation* is apart from our doing. It is the exercise of grace in His own compassionate, loving heart toward us to restore our souls and put us back into fellowship with God where we can enjoy our spiritual birthright. The moment a born again believer sins, Christ acts as Advocate, making intercession for us.

The Holy Spirit likewise acts, in that He applies the Word to convict and cleanse us from sin. We are *redeemed* by the precious blood of Jesus, and the blood cleanses us from all sin; but when the *believer* sins, it is no longer redeeming blood. Why? Because God redeems us *only once,* we are born into His family only one time. It is through the washing of the water *by the Word* that we are cleansed after we are saved.

Present: As Our Advocate

Jesus said to His disciples, "Now ye are clean *through THE WORD* which I have spoken unto you" (John 15:3). Paul explains that Christ loved the Church, "and gave Himself for it, *that He might sanctify and CLEANSE it with the washing of water by THE WORD,* that He might present it to Himself a glorious Church, not having spot, or wrinkle, or any such thing; but that it should be holy and without blemish" (Eph. 5:25–27).

It is by the Word of God (applied through the mighty power of the Holy Spirit) that the believer is convicted of sin. *Confession* of sin follows conviction, and conviction always *precedes* confession. In other words, we will never confess sin until we are convicted, and we will never *be* convicted until *the Word of God,* through the Spirit, convicts us. God restores us, but the restoration begins through the cleansing power of the Word as it is applied through the power of the Holy Spirit.

Notice also, I John 2:1 does not say, "We have an Advocate *with GOD.*" It says, "We have an Advocate *with THE FATHER.*" This is a *family* matter, a *family transaction,* if you please. The heavenly Father can do nothing but love those whom He has bought through the sufferings and death of His only begotten Son on the cross. The conception that the Father is *angry* with His sinning child is error. He is angry with the *wicked* every day, but He is not angry with His child. Some Christians believe that the Son seated at the right hand of God pleads, begs, and implores God to be merciful and forgive the believer who sins, but this is unscriptural. It is God's joy to forgive His children when our Advocate makes a plea on our behalf.

Satan is the accuser of the brethren, and this is

another reason for Christ's advocacy on our behalf. Satan still has access into the presence of God, and he accuses the sinning children of God day and night. But our Advocate, the Lord Jesus Christ, meets every one of Satan's attacks on God's people with the fact that *He* made propitiation, *He* died for our sins—and thus Satan is put to flight.

However, the day will come when Satan will no longer be free to accuse God's children. In Revelation 12:10 we read, "I heard a loud voice saying in heaven, Now is come salvation, and strength, and the kingdom of God, and the power of His Christ: *for the AC-CUSER OF OUR BRETHREN is cast down, which accused them before our God DAY AND NIGHT!*" Until then, thank God there is no one who can condemn us, no, not even Satan; for Christ Jesus stands in our stead and pleads our case. "Who is he that condemneth? It is *Christ* that died, yea rather, that is risen again, who is even at the right hand of God, who also *maketh intercession for us*" (Rom. 8:34).

His Priesthood:—

"Wherefore in all things it behoved Him to be made like unto His brethren, that He might be a merciful and faithful High Priest in things pertaining to God, to make reconciliation for the sins of the people. For in that He Himself hath suffered being tempted, He is able to succour them that are tempted" (Heb. 2:17, 18).

This passage speaks of the propitiation Christ made for the sins of the people. His suffering in our stead, His being tempted in all points as *we* are tempted, yet without sin—these facts are the basis of His *intercessory* service.

"Seeing then that we have a great High Priest, that

is passed into the heavens, Jesus the Son of God, let us hold fast our profession. For we have not an high priest which cannot be touched with the feeling of our infirmities; but was in all points tempted like as we are, yet without sin. Let us therefore come boldly unto the throne of grace, that we may obtain mercy, and find grace to help in time of need" (Heb. 4:14—16).

These verses reveal how Christ, while on earth, was fitted for the great work of His priesthood. As He tabernacled among men He endured all of the heart-aches, sufferings, and temptations to which man is subject. *But Jesus never sinned.* He faced every possible difficulty we face—and more. Therefore He can be merciful toward us, and as our faithful High Priest He can enter into our sorrows and trials, knowing our anxieties and sympathizing with us in our difficulties and conflicts. Having Himself been a Stranger in a strange land, He understands that *we* are pilgrims and strangers on earth. Our citizenship is in heaven "from whence also we look for the Saviour, the Lord Jesus Christ" (Phil. 3:20).

We must understand, however, that Christ does not intercede for the flesh, He has no sympathy with sin in the life of a believer. "They that are Christ's have *crucified the flesh* with the affections and lusts" (Gal. 5:24).

By His gracious and unbroken intercession in the sanctuary, Christ upholds believers individually, giving strength to endure and courage to stand; and if it were not for Christ's intercession for us we would fall by the wayside and utterly fail in our spiritual life! It matters not how severe the trial may be nor how sorely we may be tried, we have His promise: "There hath no temptation taken you but such as is common

99

to man: but God is faithful, who will not suffer you to be tempted above that ye are able; but will with the temptation also make a way to escape, that ye may be able to bear it" (I Cor. 10:13). Believers can claim this promise just as surely as we claim John 3:16.

I would not minimize the power of our enemy. Satan is shrewd, cunning, intelligent, and powerful. He knows how to lay snares and pitfalls as he spreads his nets for the believer. His wiles are most subtle, and without our great High Priest we would be helpless in his hands. But thank God, *"we are MORE THAN CONQUERORS through Him!"* The devil is mighty, but God is ALMIGHTY. Christ knows our need, and His eyes watch *the enemy* just as His eyes watch *us.* He saw the old serpent move in on Peter, and He said to that disciple, *"Simon, Simon, behold, Satan hath desired to have you, that he may sift you as wheat: but I HAVE PRAYED FOR THEE, that thy faith fail not . . ."* (Luke 22:31, 32). Christ knew the cunning plan Satan had conceived to ensnare Peter, and before Satan's plan could be carried out the Lord prayed for him, that his faith would not fail.

The devil did not take Peter's Lord into consideration when he schemed to ensnare that apostle. Believers have the same Lord today. *God is no respecter of persons*, therefore *Jesus* is no respecter of persons; and as He prayed for Peter, He also prays for us. *He* sees the foe *before we see him.* He prays for us before Satan can approach us, and thus we are victorious IN HIM.

In Ephesians 6:10—17 *the Apostle Paul* warns against the enemy: "Finally, my brethren, be strong in the Lord, and in the power of His might. Put on the whole armour of God, that ye may be able to stand against the wiles of the devil. For we wrestle not against flesh and blood, but against principalities, against powers, against the rulers of the darkness of this world, against spiritual wickedness in high places. Wherefore take unto you the whole armour of God, that ye may be able to withstand in the evil day, and having done all, to stand. Stand therefore, having your loins girt about with truth, and having on the breastplate of righteousness; and your feet shod with the preparation of the Gospel of peace; above all, taking the shield of faith, wherewith ye shall be able to quench all the fiery darts of the wicked. And take the helmet of salvation, and the sword of the Spirit, which is the Word of God."

We can also claim Hebrews 13:5, 6: "Let your conversation be without covetousness; and be content with such things as ye have: for He hath said, *I WILL NEVER LEAVE THEE, NOR FORSAKE THEE. So that we may boldly say, The Lord is my helper, and I will not fear what man shall do unto me.*" The question is, Do we *believe* those inspired words penned down by the Apostle Paul? Do we *truly believe* that Jesus will never leave us nor forsake us? If we believe these promises from God's Word, then we will not worry about those things which may never happen— that is, we will not borrow trouble by fretting about the future, or about threatened difficulties or tragedies that may never come to pass. If we truly believe God's promises to His children, then we will be willing to accept the blessing of Romans 8:28, and know that *"all things work together for GOOD to them that love God, to them who are the called according to HIS PURPOSE!"* There are no "accidents" in God's dealing with His people, and whatever happens to the Christian, whatever comes into our lives, is for our good and God's glory.

We will never know in this world how much we owe to this blessed present work of our Lord in glory, seated at the right hand of God. What glorious revelation will come to us when we shall know as we are known, and when from our eternal home with Him we look back and behold what the intercession of our great High Priest has accomplished for us!

Now hear this: *"By HIM therefore let us offer the sacrifice of praise to God continually, that is, the fruit of our lips giving thanks to His name"* (Heb. 13:15). Jesus not only makes intercession for us and watches over us. He also presents our spiritual sacrifices to God the Father—our worship, our prayers, our praise. You see, our worship, prayer, and praise lack perfection because *we* are imperfect. But our *perfect High Priest* takes our imperfect offerings and presents them to God, thus making them acceptable. God delights in our worship, praise, and prayers because *His Son accepts them*, and *through HIM* they are acceptable to God the Father.

Christ Knoweth His Own

"Verily, verily, I say unto you, He that entereth not by the door into the sheepfold, but climbeth up some other way, the same is a thief and a robber. But he that entereth in by the door is the shepherd of the sheep. To him the porter openeth; and the sheep hear his voice: and he calleth his own sheep by name, and leadeth them out. And when he putteth forth his own sheep, he goeth before them, and the sheep follow him: for they know his voice. And a stranger will they not follow, but will flee from him: for they know not the voice of strangers.

"This parable spake Jesus unto them: but they understood not what things they were which He spake unto them. Then said Jesus unto them again, Verily, verily, I say unto you,

I AM THE DOOR of the sheep. All that ever came before me are thieves and robbers: but the sheep did not hear them. *I AM THE DOOR: by me if any man enter in, he shall be saved,* and shall go in and out, and find pasture. The thief cometh not, but for to steal, and to kill, and to destroy: I am come that they might have life, and that they might have it more abundantly.

"*I AM THE GOOD SHEPHERD. The Good Shepherd giveth His life for the sheep.* But he that is an hireling, and not the Shepherd, whose own the sheep are not, seeth the wolf coming, and leaveth the sheep, and fleeth: and the wolf catcheth them, and scattereth the sheep. The hireling fleeth, because he is an hireling, and careth not for the sheep. *I AM THE GOOD SHEPHERD, AND KNOW MY SHEEP, AND AM KNOWN OF MINE.* As the Father knoweth me, even so know I the Father: and I lay down my life for the sheep. . . .

"Then came the Jews round about Him, and said unto Him, How long dost thou make us to doubt? If thou be the Christ, tell us plainly. Jesus answered them, I told you, and ye believed not: the works that I do in my Father's name, they bear witness of me. *But ye believe not, because YE ARE NOT OF MY SHEEP,* as I said unto you. *MY SHEEP HEAR MY VOICE, AND I KNOW THEM, AND THEY FOLLOW ME: and I give unto them eternal life; and they shall never perish, neither shall any man pluck them out of my hand.* My Father, which gave them me, is greater than all; and no man is able to pluck them out of my Father's hand" (John 10:1—15, 24—29).

"*The Lord knoweth them that are his*—what a comforting, blessed assurance! The Lord knows His children by name—and in the light of this truth all fear and unbelief should be banished from our hearts. But even more wonderful is the fact that He knew us when we wandered in sin, when we were "aliens from

103

the commonwealth of Israel, and strangers from the covenants of promise, having no hope, and without God in the world" (Eph. 2:12). *"We love Him because He first loved US"* (I John 4:19). His loving eyes followed us in our sins. He sought us in His love and brought us unto Himself through the mighty power of the Holy Spirit and the incorruptible seed of the Word of God. He gave us His life to dwell within us when we heard and embraced the Word, receiving Him by faith.

The Apostle Paul points out that each believer is the object of Christ's love. He explained to the Roman believers, "When we were yet without strength, in due time *Christ died for the ungodly. . . .* God commendeth His love toward us, in that, *WHILE WE WERE YET SINNERS, Christ died for us. MUCH MORE then, being now justified by His blood, we shall be saved from wrath through Him.* For if, when we were *enemies,* we were reconciled to God by the death of His Son, *MUCH MORE, being reconciled, we shall be saved BY HIS LIFE.* And not only so, but we also joy in God through our Lord Jesus Christ, by whom we have now received the atonement" (Rom. 5:6–11 in part).

Christ died—not for the righteous, but for the ungodly; and such were we all. Jesus Himself declared, "They that be whole need not a physician, but they that are sick. . . . I am not come to call the righteous, *but sinners,* to repentance" (Matt. 9:12, 13). In due time—in God's time—Christ died for sinners, and through faith in His finished work (justified by His blood) *"we shall be saved from wrath through Him."*

Then Paul points out that if, when we were *enemies* to God, we were reconciled to Him by the *death* of His Son, "much more, being reconciled, *we shall be*

104

saved by His LIFE." Now what "life" is meant here? It cannot be applied to the life of the Lord Jesus Christ before He died on the cross, for sinless and perfect as His earthly life was, it had no saving power for us. We could never have been saved through the righteous life Jesus lived. His purity and holiness showed us how exceedingly sinful *we* are, but it is not by His holy life that we are saved. The "life" referred to here is the life Christ now lives at the right hand of God—in other words, *Christ is living for us today,* at the right hand of the Majesty on high. So we are *kept saved* on earth because Christ lives in heaven. We need not only a *Redeemer,* but a *Saviour.* We could not redeem ourselves from the penalty of sin, and no more can we save ourselves from the *power* of sin, the daily habits of sin. Therefore we are saved *through HIS LIFE.* He is living *for us,* hallelujah! and *"there is therefore now NO CONDEMNATION to them which are in Christ Jesus,* who walk not after the flesh, but after the Spirit" (Rom. 8:1).

Hebrews 7:24, 25 tells us, "This Man (Christ), because He continueth ever, hath *an unchangeable priesthood.* Wherefore He is able also to save them to the uttermost that come unto God by Him, seeing *He ever liveth to make intercession for them."* Then in Hebrews 9:24 we read these glorious words: "For Christ is not entered into the holy places made with hands, which are the figures of the true; but *into heaven itself, now to appear IN THE PRESENCE OF GOD FOR US!"*

Beloved, Christ entered into the heaven of heavens, and God seated Him at His own right hand where He sits today to make intercession for us—but notice this is not spoken of unbelievers. The unsaved are not Christ's children, they have no share in all the truths stated here. The *unbelieving world* does not have an intercessor. Jesus Himself clearly declared this divine truth in His intercessory prayer recorded in John chapter 17. In verse 9 of that chapter Jesus said to the heavenly Father, *"I pray not for the world, but for them which thou hast given me; for they are thine."*

This same truth is foreshadowed in the Old Testament Scriptures. The high priest, dressed in garments of beauty and glory, had an onyx stone on each shoulder, twelve precious stones on his breastplate, and on each stone *names* were engraved. And *whose were the names* engraved thereon? Were they names of outstanding Egyptians—the Pharaohs, perhaps? Or names of Hittites, or Amorites, or Jebusites? Certainly not! They were the names of the twelve tribes of Israel, God's own people—and the names were *engraved* on the stones. They were not *written,* where they might be erased or blotted out. They were engraved deep into the stone, which speaks of the keeping power of God in relation to His children. Just so, *our great High Priest,* the Lord Jesus Christ, carries believers upon His shoulders and upon His bosom. We are safe in His care, protected by His power and led by His nail-scarred hands. Each believing soul is one spirit with the Lord, and He knows us much better than we know ourselves. He knows our every difficulty, temptation, and trial. He knows our conflicts, He sees every tear that falls from our eyes.

The Psalmist wrote, "The steps of a good man are ordered by the Lord: and he delighteth in His way. . . . The salvation of the righteous is of the Lord: He is their strength in the time of trouble. And the Lord shall help them, and deliver them: He shall deliver them from the wicked, and save them, because they trust in Him" (Psalm 37:23, 39, 40).

"As far as the east is from the west, so far hath He removed our transgressions from us. Like as a father pitieth his children, so the Lord pitieth them that fear Him. *For He knoweth our frame; He remembereth that we are dust"* (Psalm 103:12—14).

God's eye is upon every believer—the eye that measures the depths of the universe and sees every sparrow that falls. Our God neither slumbers nor sleeps (Psalm 121:3, 4). The multiplied millions of His people who have passed through this life and are now with Him in glory were each and individually the object of His love and care until they were safely home with Him. His loving eye was upon the multitudes of martyrs who were burned at the stake, broken on the torture rack, or fed to wild beasts in the arena. For each of these martyrs Christ served and worked—and He serves and works for us today. He is our Representative before God the Father, and He will continue in that work until we are safe in His arms in Paradise.

This precious truth should encourage us to live a life of prayer in this present world. We are surrounded by evil, danger lurks on every hand, Satan is ever on the alert to ensnare us. Paul exhorted the Philippian believers, *"Be careful for nothing;* but *in every thing* by prayer and supplication with thanksgiving *let your requests be made known unto God.* And the peace of God, which passeth all understanding, shall keep your hearts and minds through Christ Jesus" (Phil. 4:6, 7).

Since Christ is interested in everything that happens to the believer, no matter how small or how great the happening may be, we can go to Him in prayer and talk with Him as freely as we would talk with our parents, with our family doctor, or with our church pastor. He listens to our every request, He knows what we have need of even before we ask, and He joys to share in all that we do. Just as His eyes are open to watch over us, His ears are attuned to our prayers. He understands our discouragement, our weariness, our sorrows and hardships. He passed this way before He asked us to walk this pilgrimage. He knows and sympathizes when we are lonely, when our dedicated service to Him is misunderstood by our fellowman, and when the fiery darts of the wicked are aimed at us.

Believers today can claim the promise Jesus made to His disciples in John 15:7: *"IF YE ABIDE IN ME, AND MY WORDS ABIDE IN YOU, ye shall ask what ye will, and it shall be done unto you!"*

Practical Results of Christ's Present Work In the Believer's Life

"Know ye not that ye are the temple of God, and that the Spirit of God dwelleth in you?" (I Cor. 3:16).

"What? Know ye not that your body is the temple of the Holy Ghost which is in you, which ye have of God, and ye are not your own? For ye are bought with a price: therefore glorify God in your body, and in your spirit, which are God's" (I Cor. 6:19, 20).

What a vast change would come into our daily lives if we would remember constantly that Jesus sees every move we make, hears every word we say, and knows every thought that passes through our mind! If we would remember that He is present with us each moment of each day, many things we do would be left undone, many words we speak would remain unspoken, and many subjects on which our thoughts now dwell would be put aside. He is our Representative before God, and we are *His* representatives before *men.* Therefore our words and actions make up a testimony either *for* Christ or *against* Him before unbelievers. If our lives bring honor and glory to God, we will lead others to know the Lord Jesus Christ as Saviour; but if we dishonor God by participating in things of the world and living as the world lives, unbelievers will see nothing in us to cause them to thirst for the living water or hunger after righteousness.

In Christ we live and move and have our being. The branch severed from the vine cannot bear fruit. We live because Jesus lives, we have victory because He came forth victorious. He is heir of all things, therefore in Him we too are heirs of God and joint-heirs with Christ. Since God, through His beloved Son, has done so much for us, it is our duty to honor Him with all that we have and all that we are. As Paul admonished the Corinthians, *"Whether therefore ye eat, or drink, or whatsoever ye do, DO ALL TO THE GLORY OF GOD"* (I Cor. 10:31).

Paul also reminded young Titus that the grace of God that *saves* us also *teaches* us "that denying ungodliness and worldly lusts, we should live soberly, righteously, and godly, in this present world, looking for that blessed hope, and the glorious appearing of the great God and our Saviour Jesus Christ" (Tit. 2:11—13).

God gave His best for us. He gave the sacrifice of His only begotten Son. Now He wants *us*—not to die for Him, but to *live* for Him, presenting our bodies "a *living* sacrifice, holy, acceptable unto God," which is our reasonable service. He wants us to "be not conformed to this world," but *transformed* by the renewing of our mind, that we may prove "what is that good, and acceptable, and perfect, *will of God"*

(Rom. 12:1, 2).

Christ's Present Work For the Church

"The husband is the head of the wife, even as Christ is the head of the Church: and He is the Saviour of the body. Therefore as the Church is subject unto Christ, so let the wives be to their own husbands in every thing. Husbands, love your wives, even as Christ also loved the Church, and gave Himself for it; that He might sanctify and cleanse it with the washing of water by the Word, that He might present it to Himself a glorious Church, not having spot, or wrinkle, or any such thing; but that it should be holy and without blemish.

"So ought men to love their wives as their own bodies. He that loveth his wife loveth himself. For no man ever yet hated his own flesh; but nourisheth and cherisheth it, even as the Lord the Church: for we are members of His body, of His flesh, and of His bones. For this cause shall a man leave his father and mother, and shall be joined unto his wife, and they two shall be one flesh. This is a great mystery: but I speak concerning Christ and the Church" (Eph. 5:23—32).

"Other foundation can no man lay than that is laid, which is Jesus Christ" (I Cor. 3:11).

So we see that Christ is the head and the foundation of the New Testament Church, the Church is His body, and *every born again believer* is a *member* of that body. The risen Lord adds new members to the Church daily, putting each believer into the body as it pleases Him. He also supplies the body with various *gifts* as it pleases Him. Paul explains this very carefully and completely in his letter to the Corinthian church:

110

"Now concerning spiritual gifts, brethren, I would not have you ignorant. Ye know that ye were Gentiles, carried away unto these dumb idols, even as ye were led. Wherefore I give you to understand, that no man speaking by the Spirit of God calleth Jesus accursed: and that no man can say that Jesus is the Lord, but by the Holy Ghost.

"Now there are diversities of gifts, but the same Spirit. And there are differences of administrations, but the same Lord. And there are diversities of operations, but it is the same God which worketh all in all. But the manifestation of the Spirit is given to every man to profit withal. For to one is given by the Spirit the word of wisdom; to another the word of knowledge by the same Spirit; to another faith by the same Spirit; to another the gifts of healing by the same Spirit; to another the working of miracles; to another prophecy; to another discerning of spirits; to another divers kinds of tongues; to another the interpretation of tongues: but all these worketh that one and the selfsame Spirit, dividing to every man severally as He will.

"For as the body is one, and hath many members, and all the members of that one body, being many, are one body: so also is Christ. For by one Spirit are we all baptized into one body, whether we be Jews or Gentiles, whether we be bond or free; and have been all made to drink into one Spirit. For the body is not one member, but many. If the foot shall say, Because I am not the hand, I am not of the body; is it therefore not of the body? And if the ear shall say, Because I am not the eye, I am not of the body; is it therefore not of the body? If the whole body were an eye, where were the hearing? If the whole were hearing, where were the smelling?

"But now hath God set the members every one of them in the body, as it hath pleased Him. And if they were all one member, where were the body? But now are they many members, yet but one body. And the eye cannot say unto the hand, I have no need of thee: nor again the head to the

111

feet, I have no need of you. Nay, much more those members of the body, which seem to be more feeble, are necessary: and those members of the body, which we think to be less honourable, upon these we bestow more abundant honour; and our uncomely parts have more abundant comeliness. For our comely parts have no need: but God hath tempered the body together, having given more abundant honour to that part which lacked: that there should be no schism in the body; but that the members should have the same care one for another. And whether one member suffer, all the members suffer with it; or one member be honoured, all the members rejoice with it.

"Now ye are the body of Christ, and members in particular. And God hath set some in the Church, first apostles, secondarily prophets, thirdly teachers, after that miracles, then gifts of healings, helps, governments, diversities of tongues. Are all apostles? Are all prophets? Are all teachers? Are all workers of miracles? Have all the gifts of healing? Do all speak with tongues? Do all interpret? But covet earnestly the best gifts: and yet shew I unto you a more excellent way" (I Cor. 12: 1—31).

In Ephesians 4:11—16 we also learn of the diversities of gifts given to the Church, and the *purpose* of the giving: "He gave some, apostles; and some, prophets; and some, evangelists; and some, pastors and teachers; *for the perfecting of the saints, for the work of the ministry, for the edifying of the body of Christ: till we all come in the unity of the faith, and of the knowledge of the Son of God, unto a perfect man, unto the measure of the stature of the fulness of Christ:* That we henceforth be no more children, tossed to and fro, and carried about with every wind of doctrine, by the sleight of men, and cunning craftiness, whereby they lie in wait to deceive; but speaking the truth in love, may grow up into Him in all things, which is the head, even Christ: from whom the whole body fitly joined together and compacted by that which every joint supplieth, according to the effectual working in the measure of every part, maketh increase of the body unto the edifying of itself in love."

To the Church God gives apostles, prophets, evangelists, pastors, teachers—and these are given "for the *perfecting of the saints,* for the *work of the ministry,* for the *edifying* of the body of Christ, till we all come in the unity of the faith, and of the knowledge of the Son of God, *unto a PERFECT MAN."* Some day the Church, the body of Christ, will be complete—and what happens then? *Then* we come "unto the measure of the stature of the fulness of Christ."

This will occur when we are caught up to meet Him in the clouds in the air, when we see Him as He is and shall be like Him. His *present work* in behalf of His own will be finished when we are caught up to meet Him, when we are taken out of this wilderness of sin and brought home to the Father's house. At that time there will be no further need for His power and love to sustain us. We will have a body like unto His glorious resurrection body. We will be with Him in the celestial city where no tears will be shed and where there will be no more pain, no more sorrow, no more dying.

Our Advocate will not need to exercise His powers of advocacy then, for we will have been delivered forever from the presence of sin. We will be sanctified wholly—soul, spirit, and body. Then and only then will sinning be impossible. Oh, happy day when that day finally arrives!

Believers Share In Christ's Work

"I am the true vine, and my Father is the husbandman. Every branch in me that beareth not fruit He taketh away: and every branch that beareth fruit, He purgeth it, that it may bring forth more fruit. Now ye are clean through the word which I have spoken unto you. Abide in me, and I in you. As the branch cannot bear fruit of itself, except it abide in the vine; no more can ye, except ye abide in me. I am the vine, ye are the branches: He that abideth in me, and I in him, the same bringeth forth much fruit: for without me ye can do nothing. . . . Henceforth I call you not servants; for the servant knoweth not what his lord doeth: but I have called you friends; for all things that I have heard of my Father I have made known unto you. Ye have not chosen me, but I have chosen you, and ordained you, that ye should go and bring forth fruit, and that your fruit should remain: that whatsoever ye shall ask of the Father in my name, He may give it you. These things I command you, that ye love one another" (John 15:1−5, 15−17).

Yes, Christ permits us to have some share in this blessed work He is now doing for believers. He prayed for us, and we can pray for one another. We *should* pray for *all saints*—that is, Christ intercedes for us, and we should intercede for our fellow believers.

Christ washed the disciples' feet, thus setting an example of humility and service. We should wash one another's feet—literally if need be, but more especially in humble service, helping each other as brothers and sisters in Christ. He carries our burdens, therefore we should share in bearing the burdens of our fellow Christians.

Christ forgives and restores us. Certainly we should forgive our brother if he sins against us, even as our blessed Lord forgave us. Paul tells us, "Put on, therefore, as the elect of God, holy and beloved, bowels of

114

mercies, kindness, humbleness of mind, meekness, long-suffering; forbearing one another, and forgiving one another, if any man have a quarrel against any: even as Christ forgave you, so also do ye" (Col. 3:12, 13).

Paul exhorted the Galatian believers, "Brethren, if a man be overtaken in a fault, ye which are spiritual, restore such an one in the spirit of meekness; considering thyself, lest thou also be tempted. Bear ye one another's burdens, and so fulfil the law of Christ. For if a man think himself to be something, when he is nothing, he deceiveth himself. But let every man prove his own work, and then shall he have rejoicing in himself alone, and not in another. For every man shall bear his own burden. Let him that is taught in the Word communicate unto him that teacheth in all good things" (Gal. 6:1—6).

In Paul's instructions to the Ephesian church he wrote, "Be ye kind one to another, tenderhearted, forgiving one another, even as God *for Christ's sake* hath forgiven you" (Eph. 4:32).

It is a grand and glorious privilege to be a child of God, but the privilege carries grave and weighty responsibilities. If we fail to walk in the footsteps of Jesus in service, we will lose our reward. All believers are members of the body of Christ; and as members of the same body we should love our Christian brethren as Christ loved us. Then when opportunity presents itself we should do what we can to help other believers, to share their burdens, to encourage and uphold the weak.

We are instructed to "be not drunk with wine, wherein is excess; but be filled with the Spirit; speaking to yourselves in psalms and hymns and spiritual songs, singing and making melody in your heart to the Lord; giving thanks always for all things unto

God and the Father in the name of our Lord Jesus Christ; *submitting yourselves one to another in the fear of God"* (Eph. 5:18—21).

We are also instructed, *"Rejoice evermore. Pray without ceasing"* (I Thess. 5:16,17). If we rejoice in the Lord, if we live continually in an attitude of prayer, making our requests known unto God, there will be no room in our hearts and minds for worry, anxiety, and fear. These are actually accusations against Christ, as Martha accused Him when she was "cumbered about much serving" and she said to Jesus, *"Lord, dost thou not CARE . . . ?"* Jesus *did* care—but He was concerned about the major things while Martha was troubled about the minor. Therefore He answered, "Martha, Martha, thou art careful and troubled about many things: but one thing is needful: and Mary hath chosen that good part, which shall not be taken away from her" (Luke 10:40—42).

We need not be "careful and troubled" about things. God has promised to care for us and to supply our needs. The trusting Christian can say with Paul, *"I can do ALL things through Christ which strengtheneth me. . . . My God shall supply ALL your need according to His riches in glory by Christ Jesus"* (Phil. 4:13,19).

Let us commit to memory and engrave upon our hearts the words of the Psalmist: "Commit thy way unto the Lord; trust also in Him; and HE shall bring it to pass!" (Psalm 37:5).

Chapter III

CHRIST'S FUTURE WORK

"Behold, the day of the Lord cometh, and thy spoil shall be divided in the midst of thee. For I will gather all nations against Jerusalem to battle; and the city shall be taken, and the houses rifled, and the women ravished; and half of the city shall go forth into captivity, and the residue of the people shall not be cut off from the city.

"Then shall the Lord go forth, and fight against those nations, as when He fought in the day of battle. And His feet shall stand in that day upon the Mount of Olives, which is before Jerusalem on the east, and the Mount of Olives shall cleave in the midst thereof toward the east and toward the west, and there shall be a very great valley; and half of the mountain shall remove toward the north, and half of it toward the south. And ye shall flee to the valley of the mountains; for the valley of the mountains shall reach unto Azal: yea, ye shall flee, like as ye fled from before the earthquake in the days of Uzziah king of Judah: and the Lord my God shall come, and all the saints with thee.

"And it shall come to pass in that day, that the light shall not be clear, nor dark: but it shall be one day which shall be known to the Lord, not day, nor night: but it shall come to pass, that at evening time it shall be light. And it shall be in that day, that living waters shall go out from Jerusalem; half of them toward the former sea, and half of them toward the hinder sea: in summer and in winter shall it be. *AND THE LORD SHALL BE KING OVER ALL THE EARTH: in that day shall there be ONE LORD, and His name one"* (Zech. 14:1—9).

The Lord Jesus Christ finished the work of redemption, He is now bodily present at the right hand of the Majesty on high, exercising His priesthood in behalf of believers on earth. But our Redeemer and great High Priest is also King, and one day He will rule over all the earth. To Him belongeth a kingdom, and one day He will possess that kingdom. He will be King on a throne and He will receive kingly glory.

Yes, Christ has a future work, a kingly work, to do. His *past* work was foretold by the Spirit of God in the Old Testament Scriptures. His *priestly* work is *foreshadowed* in the Old Testament in many, many ways and *fulfilled* in the New Testament. In like manner, both the Old and the New Testaments speak of His future work as King of kings and Lord of lords, and of His glorious kingdom on earth (Heb. 1:1—3).

Jesus Announced King of the Earth

"He shall be great, and shall be called the Son of the Highest: and the Lord God shall give unto Him the throne of His father David: and He shall reign over the house of Jacob for ever; and of His kingdom there shall be no end" (Luke 1:32, 33).

The angel Gabriel announced Christ's kingly work when he told the Virgin Mary that she would be the mother of God's only begotten Son. According to the message of Gabriel, Christ *must* occupy the throne of David and He *must reign* and possess the kingdom. The entire prophetic Word has its climax in the vision of the King and His glorious kingdom here on earth.

In His first advent Christ was despised and rejected

of men, a Man of sorrows and acquainted with grief,
brutally crucified on a Roman cross; but the scriptural
prophecies of His glory to come are the glittering stars
that shine throughout the dark night of this present
age.   The day is coming when Jesus *will be King*
over all the earth.   The prophecies concerning the
King and His kingdom give us assurance, inspire hope
and courage.   Shall we look first at some of the many
passages in the Old Testament which clearly declare
Him as King and assure us that He will one day
possess His kingdom?

In Psalm 2:1—12 we read: "Why do the heathen
rage, and the people imagine a vain thing? The kings
of the earth set themselves, and the rulers take counsel
together, against the Lord, and against His anointed,
saying, Let us break their bands asunder, and cast
away their cords from us. He that sitteth in the heavens shall laugh: the Lord shall have them in derision.

"Then shall He speak unto them in His wrath, and
vex them in His sore displeasure. Yet have I set my
King upon my holy hill of Zion. I will declare the
decree: the Lord hath said unto me, Thou art my
Son; this day have I begotten thee. Ask of me, and I
shall give thee the heathen for thine inheritance, and
the uttermost parts of the earth for thy possession.
Thou shalt break them with a rod of iron; thou shalt
dash them in pieces like a potter's vessel.

"Be wise now therefore, O ye kings: be instructed,
ye judges of the earth. Serve the Lord with fear, and
rejoice with trembling. Kiss the Son, lest He be angry, and ye perish from the way, when His wrath is
kindled but a little. Blessed are all they that put their
trust in Him."

Certainly the heathen are raging today, and the
people "imagine a vain thing"—they imagine that they

119

will conquer outer space and inhabit the moon and the planets. Like Nimrod of old, they are attempting to build a tower to God's heaven! But the Lord God Almighty, "He that sitteth in the heavens," shall laugh and shall have them in derision. Psalm 115:16 declares, *"The heaven, even the heavens, are the Lord's,* but the *earth* hath He given *to the children of men."*

In Psalm 9:1—8 the Psalmist wrote, "I will praise thee, O Lord, with my whole heart; I will shew forth all thy marvellous works. I will be glad and rejoice in thee: I will sing praise to thy name, O thou most High. When mine enemies are turned back, they shall fall and perish at thy presence. For thou hast maintained my right and my cause; thou satest in the throne judging right. Thou hast rebuked the heathen, thou hast destroyed the wicked, thou hast put out their name for ever and ever. O thou enemy, destructions are come to a perpetual end: and thou hast destroyed cities; their memorial is perished with them. BUT THE LORD SHALL ENDURE FOR EVER: HE HATH PREPARED HIS THRONE FOR JUDGMENT. And He shall judge the world IN RIGHTEOUSNESS, He shall minister judgment to the people IN UPRIGHTNESS."

When King Jesus sits on the throne of David and rules over this earth, then will be the Utopia about which man has talked and for which he has planned but has never been able to bring about. Jesus the righteous King will judge the world in righteousness, and every man will receive exactly what he deserves— no more and no less. There is a day coming when we will have world peace—the peace so talked about today, but never experienced. When the King of glory sits on the throne of David, *then* will be the time when men will beat their swords into plowshares and their spears into pruning hooks!

Who IS the King of glory? The Psalmist settles that question: "Lift up your heads, O ye gates; even lift them up, ye everlasting doors; and the King of glory shall come in. Who is this King of glory? *THE LORD OF HOSTS, He is the King of glory!*" (Psalm 24:9, 10).

"O clap your hands, all ye people; shout unto God with the voice of triumph. For the Lord most high is terrible; *He is a great King over all the earth.* He shall subdue the people under us, and the nations under our feet. He shall choose our inheritance for us, the excellency of Jacob whom He loved.

"God is gone up with a shout, the Lord with the sound of a trumpet. Sing praises to God, sing praises: sing praises *unto our King,* sing praises. *For GOD IS THE KING OF ALL THE EARTH:* sing ye praises with understanding. *God reigneth over the heathen: God sitteth upon the throne of His holiness.* The princes of the people are gathered together, even the people of the God of Abraham: for the shields of the earth belong unto God: *He is greatly exalted*" (Psalm 47).

Here is the cry of victory! Clap your hands, all ye people—*GOD is King over all the earth!* The throne of David is a historical throne as surely as the throne of the Caesars was a historical throne, and one day the King of glory will sit on that throne and reign over the whole earth. "All kings shall fall down before Him: all nations shall serve Him. . . . His name shall endure for ever: His name shall be continued as long as the sun: and men shall be blessed in Him: all nations shall call Him blessed" (Psalm 72:11, 17). Yes, the King of kings will be *"higher than the kings of the earth"* (Psalm 89:27).

The following prophecies from the Old Testament also apply to Christ's reign on earth:

Isaiah 32:1: "Behold, a King shall reign *in righteousness,* and princes shall rule in judgment."

Jeremiah 23:5, 6: "Behold, the days come, saith the Lord, that I will raise unto David a righteous Branch, and a King shall reign and prosper, and shall execute judgment and justice in the earth. In His days Judah shall be saved, and Israel shall dwell safely: *and this is His name whereby He shall be called, THE LORD OUR RIGHTEOUSNESS."*

Daniel 7:13, 14: "I saw in the night visions, and, behold, One like the Son of man came with the clouds of heaven, and came to the Ancient of days, and they brought Him near before Him. And there was given Him dominion, and glory, and a kingdom, that all people, nations, and languages, should serve Him: *His dominion is an everlasting dominion, which shall not pass away, and His kingdom that which shall not be destroyed."*

Zechariah 6:12, 13: "And speak unto him, saying, Thus speaketh the Lord of hosts, saying, Behold the Man whose name is The BRANCH; and He shall grow up out of His place, and He shall build the temple of the Lord: Even He shall build the temple of the Lord; and He shall bear the glory, and shall sit and rule upon His throne; and He shall be a Priest upon His throne: and the counsel of peace shall be between them both."

To me, the greatest passage concerning the kingdom of God on earth and the reign of Christ is found in Isaiah 9:6, 7: *"Unto us a Child is born, unto us a Son is given: and the government shall be upon His shoulder: and His name shall be called Wonderful,*

Counsellor, The mighty God, The everlasting Father, The Prince of Peace. Of the increase of His government and peace there shall be no end, upon the throne of David, and upon His kingdom, to order it, and to establish it with judgment and with justice from henceforth even for ever. The zeal of the Lord of hosts will perform this."

These prophecies have not yet been fulfilled. Certainly Christ did not sit on the throne of David before He went to Calvary, nor has He occupied the throne of David since He died on the cross. Men have not yet beat their swords into plowshares and their spears into pruning hooks — and every honest-hearted person knows there is no peace on earth today except in the hearts of the believing children of God! The Lord Jesus Christ has not yet begun His work as King of kings and Lord of lords. The kingdom promised to Him will be given to Him, literally, but He has not yet received it from the heavenly Father. But *there will be* such a kingdom on earth, when Jesus returns in the Revelation, when He stands on the Mount of Olives, when He judges the Antichrist and his armies and then takes up His reign from the throne of David. Righteousness and knowledge of the Lord will then cover this earth as the waters now cover the sea.

The Prophet Isaiah tells us something of this glorious kingdom which is to be set up when Jesus reigns on earth:

"There shall come forth a rod out of the stem of Jesse, and a Branch shall grow out of his roots: and the Spirit of the Lord shall rest upon Him, the Spirit of wisdom and understanding, the Spirit of counsel and might, the Spirit of knowledge and of the fear of the Lord; and shall make Him of quick understanding in the fear of the Lord: and He shall not judge after the sight of His eyes, neither reprove after the hearing

123

of His ears: But with righteousness shall He judge the poor, and reprove with equity for the meek of the earth: and He shall smite the earth with the rod of His mouth, and with the breath of His lips shall He slay the wicked. And righteousness shall be the girdle of His loins, and faithfulness the girdle of His reins.

"The wolf also shall dwell with the lamb, and the leopard shall lie down with the kid; and the calf and the young lion and the fatling together; and a little child shall lead them. And the cow and the bear shall feed; their young ones shall lie down together: and the lion shall eat straw like the ox. And the sucking child shall play on the hole of the asp, and the weaned child shall put his hand on the cockatrice' den. They shall not hurt nor destroy in all my holy mountain: for the earth shall be full of the knowledge of the Lord, as the waters cover the sea. And in that day there shall be a root of Jesse, which shall stand for an ensign of the people; to it shall the Gentiles seek: and His rest shall be glorious" (Isa. 11:1—10).

New Testament Prophecies Concerning the King and His Kingdom On Earth

"When the Son of man shall come in His glory, and all the holy angels with Him, then shall He sit upon the throne of His glory" (Matt. 25:31).

"And as they heard these things, He added and spake a parable, because He was nigh to Jerusalem, and because they thought that the kingdom of God should immediately appear. He said therefore:

"A certain nobleman went into a far country to receive for himself a kingdom, and to return. And he called his ten servants, and delivered them ten pounds, and said unto them, Occupy till I come. But his citizens hated him, and sent a message after him, saying, We will not have this man to reign over us.

"And it came to pass, that when he was returned, having received the kingdom, then he commanded these servants to be called unto him, to whom he had given the money, that he might know how much every man had gained by trading.

"Then came the first, saying, Lord, thy pound hath gained ten pounds. And he said unto him, Well, thou good servant: because thou hast been faithful in a very little, have thou authority over ten cities. And the second came, saying, Lord, thy pound hath gained five pounds. And he said likewise to him, Be thou also over five cities. And another came, saying, Lord, behold, here is thy pound, which I have kept laid up in a napkin: for I feared thee, because thou art an austere man: thou takest up that thou layedst not down, and reapest that thou didst not sow.

"And he saith unto him, Out of thine own mouth will I judge thee, thou wicked servant. Thou knewest that I was an austere man, taking up that I laid not down, and reaping that I did not sow: Wherefore then gavest not thou my money into the bank, that at my coming I might have required mine own with usury? And he said unto them that stood by, Take from him the pound, and give it to him that hath ten pounds.

"(And they said unto him, Lord, he hath ten pounds.) For I say unto you, That unto every one which hath shall be given; and from him that hath not, even that he hath shall be taken away from him. But those mine enemies, which would not that I should reign over them, bring hither, and slay them before me.

"And when He had thus spoken, He went before, ascending up to Jerusalem" (Luke 19:11—28).

Many people—including some preachers, teachers, and evangelists—declare that *the Church* is the kingdom in which the Lord Jesus Christ rules as King, and that the Old Testament prophecies concerning the

125

kingdom glories are realized in a *spiritual* sense in the Church today. This is the doctrine of *men*. Nowhere in the Word of God is the Church called the kingdom, and nowhere in the Word do we find the Lord Jesus Christ called King of the Church! The Church is the *body* of Christ, not His kingdom.

There is a vast difference between the *kingdom of God* (which is within the hearts of believers) and the *kingdom of heaven* (which will be right here on earth). *"The kingdom of heaven"* in the Greek reads "the kingdom *of the heavens."* That term is found primarily in the Gospel of Matthew and it speaks of the reign of Christ right here on earth. It is called "the kingdom of the heavens" because it is the rule of heaven over the earth (Matt. 6:10). The expression *"kingdom of heaven"* is derived from the prophecy of Daniel where it is clearly defined as the kingdom which the *God of heaven* will set up after the Gentile world powers are destroyed by "the stone cut out of the mountain without hands." (Read Daniel 2:34, 35, 44, 45; 7:23—27.) The Gentile systems will be destroyed and the "Stone"—the Lord Jesus Christ—will sit on the throne of David and will *fill the whole earth*—with righteousness and with the knowledge of the Lord. This is the kingdom which God promised to the seed of David (II Sam. 7:8—10). This kingdom is also set forth in Zechariah 12:8 and confirmed to Jesus, the Christ, in Gabriel's message to Mary as quoted in Luke 1:32, 33.

The prayer commonly referred to as *"the Lord's prayer"* is actually *the Kingdom Prayer:* "Our Father which art in heaven, Hallowed be thy name. *Thy KINGDOM come. Thy WILL be done in EARTH, as it is in heaven.* Give us this day our daily bread. And forgive us our debts, as we forgive our debtors.

126

And lead us not into temptation, but deliver us from evil: *For thine is the kingdom, and the power, and the glory, for ever.* Amen" (Matt. 6:9—13).

Whereas the "kingdom of the heavens" is a literal kingdom and will be right here on earth, *the "kingdom of GOD"* is a spiritual kingdom. When the Pharisees demanded that Jesus tell them when the kingdom of God would come, He replied, "The kingdom of God cometh not with observation: neither shall they say, Lo here! or, lo there! for, behold, *the kingdom of God is WITHIN YOU!"* (Luke 17:20, 21).

The kingdom of God is entered only by the new birth. Jesus said to Nicodemus, "Except a man be *born again,* he cannot see the kingdom of God" (John 3:3). The kingdom of God is spiritual—not the literal reign of Christ on earth, but *Christ IN the individual by faith,* and the individual *in Christ.* We should never confuse the kingdom of heaven with the Church of the living God. But there *will be* a literal kingdom on earth. That kingdom will come after the Rapture of the Church. Jesus will reign in righteousness, and the Church, the bride of Christ, will reign with Him during the Kingdom Age when this earth will be one great Garden of Eden, a literal Paradise.

At this present time Christ occupies the Father's throne, but that is not His permanent place. He is to have His own throne during the Kingdom Age, but now He waits in heaven, "from henceforth expecting till His enemies be made His footstool" (Heb. 10:13). Yes, all things *will be* put under Him and His enemies *will become* His footstool—but that has not happened yet (Heb. 2:8). The present kingdoms of this world do not make up the kingdom of heaven. Satan, the prince of the power of the air, is king of the nations of earth today—that is, the vast majority of world

127

rulers are children of Satan rather than children of God. But the day is coming when heaven will shout, *"The kingdoms of this world are become THE KINGDOMS OF OUR LORD, AND OF HIS CHRIST; and He shall reign for ever and ever!"* (Rev. 11:15). When the seventh angel sounds his trumpet, when heaven opens and Christ appears as King of kings crowned with many crowns, then will He receive the nations for His inheritance:

"And I saw heaven opened, and behold a white horse; and He that sat upon him was called Faithful and True, and in righteousness He doth judge and make war. His eyes were as a flame of fire, and on His head were many crowns; and He had a name written that no man knew, but He Himself. And He was clothed with a vesture dipped in blood: and His name is called The Word of God.

"And the armies which were in heaven followed Him upon white horses, clothed in fine linen, white and clean. And out of His mouth goeth a sharp sword, that with it He should smite the nations: and He shall rule them with a rod of iron: and He treadeth the winepress of the fierceness and wrath of Almighty God. And He hath on His vesture and on His thigh a name written: KING OF KINGS, AND LORD OF LORDS" (Rev. 19:11—16).

The Beginning of Christ's Future Work: The Rapture of the Saints

"I would not have you to be ignorant, brethren, concerning them which are asleep, that ye sorrow not, even as others which have no hope. For if we believe that Jesus died and rose again, even so them also which sleep in Jesus will God bring with Him. For this we say unto you by the word of the Lord, that

128

we which are alive and remain unto the coming of the Lord shall not prevent them which are asleep.

"*For THE LORD HIMSELF shall descend from heaven with a SHOUT, with the voice of the archangel, and with the trump of God:* and the dead in Christ shall rise first: Then we which are alive and remain shall be *caught up together with them in the clouds, to meet the Lord in the air: and so shall we ever be with the Lord.* Wherefore comfort one another with these words" (I Thess. 4:13—18).

This Scripture contains a great and unique revelation which is completely unknown in Old Testament Scriptures. Jesus promised His disciples, "I go and prepare a place for you, *I will COME AGAIN, and receive you unto myself,* that where I am, there ye may be also" (John 14:3)—but He did not tell them in what manner He would *keep* His promise. The details of His coming for His own are given in the passage just quoted from Paul's first epistle to the Thessalonians.

Notice: The Lord *Himself* will descend from heaven—"*with a shout.*" When He accomplished *His work on the cross* He gave a shout: "*It is FINISHED!*" (Read Matthew 27:50; Mark 15:37; Luke 23:46; John 19:30.) As the risen Christ, He met His beloved ones and said to them, "*All hail*"—which in the Greek is but one word, "*chairete,*" meaning literally "*Oh, Joy!*" (Matt. 28:9). This then is the *resurrection* shout of the risen Lord, the shout of joy and victory; and when He descends in the clouds to call us up to meet Him He will *call* us with a shout.

The risen Christ passed through the heavens in His glorious ascension and entered into the very presence of Almighty God. One day—it may be very, very soon—He will rise from His place at the right hand of the

Majesty on high and will descend into the first heaven just above us, to call His own to meet Him in the air. This is the blessed hope and destiny of all who have received eternal life through faith in the finished work of Christ at Calvary.

"The dead in Christ shall rise first." Immediately following the shout from heaven, the righteous dead will be raised *incorruptible*—both Old and New Testament saints. "Then we which are *alive and remain shall be caught up together with them* in the clouds, to meet the Lord in the air." Living saints will be changed "in a moment, in the twinkling of an eye, . . . For this corruptible must put on incorruption, and this mortal must put on immortality" (I Cor. 15:52, 53). Thus will every believer be caught up to meet the Lord in the air.

Some people—both ministers and laymen—teach that not all believers will be caught up in the Rapture, but the Word of God clearly declares that the Holy Spirit baptizes all believers into *one body*, the New Testament Church which is the body of Christ. Therefore when Christ comes for His Church He will call the *entire Church*, not just part of it.

The same truth is taught in John 11:25, 26 where Jesus said to Martha, *"I am the resurrection, and the life: he that believeth in me, though he were dead, yet shall he live* (in the resurrection). *And whosoever liveth* (when the Rapture comes) *and believeth in me shall never die.* (Living believers will be changed, they will not die.) *Believest thou this?"*

As for *me*, I say, *"Yes, Lord, I believe this!"* I am looking forward to that glorious morning when we will be called to meet the Lord in the air. I confess I do not understand all details of the Rapture—an event that will come suddenly and be over in a split

130

second. But it is not necessary that I understand all about it. On the basis of God's infallible Word I believe in the pre-millennial coming of Christ and the Rapture of the saints. This is *"that blessed hope"* spoken of in Titus 2:11—13. This is the beginning of Christ's future work.

The Judgment Seat of Christ

"The Father judgeth no man, but hath committed all judgment unto the Son" (John 5:22).

The Rapture, the meeting of the saints in the presence of the Lord, will be immediately followed by the judgment seat of Christ where all believers must appear to receive their rewards and give an account of deeds done in the body. Romans 14:10—12 tells us, *"We shall all stand before the judgment seat of Christ. For it is written, As I live, saith the Lord, every knee shall bow to me, and every tongue shall confess to God. So then every one of us shall give account of himself to God."* Then in II Corinthians 5:10 we read, *"We must all appear before the judgment seat of Christ; that every one may receive the things done in his body, according to that he hath done, whether it be good or bad."*

Up to this present moment no judgment has been handed down by the Lord Jesus Christ, nor have His people received their crowns and rewards for faithful stewardship and service. The Scriptures clearly teach that each believer will receive his just reward—and yes, there will be degrees of reward in heaven. Some will receive a *full* reward, some will receive a *partial* reward, and—sad but true—still others will receive *no reward at all.* This Bible fact is set forth in I Corinthians 3:11—15:

"For other foundation can no man lay than that is

131

laid, which is Jesus Christ. Now if any man build upon this foundation gold, silver, precious stones, wood, hay, stubble; every man's work shall be made manifest: for the day shall declare it, because it shall revealed by fire; and the fire shall try every man's work of what sort it is.

"If any man's work abide which he hath built thereupon, he shall receive a reward. If any man's work shall be burned, he shall suffer loss—*but he himself shall be saved, yet so AS BY FIRE!*"

We see here that there is but *ONE Foundation,* which is the Lord Jesus Christ. But men *build* upon this foundation. They can build gold, silver, precious stones; or they can build wood, hay, and stubble. At the judgment seat of Christ our works shall be tried by fire, and if our works are burned we will have no reward. Notice this does not say that fire will try our *salvation*—oh, no. It is our *works* that will be tried by fire, and it is our *works* that will be *burned* if we have built of the wrong material. However, the person whose works are burned will not be damned in the lake of fire, for our Scripture says, *"he himself shall be SAVED*—yet so as by fire."

John the Beloved also gives warning that sheds light on our rewards—or *failure* to receive a reward:

"Many deceivers are entered into the world, who confess not that Jesus Christ is come in the flesh. This is a deceiver and an antichrist. Look to yourselves, *that we LOSE NOT those things which we have wrought,* but that we receive *a full reward.* Whosoever transgresseth, and abideth not in the doctrine of Christ, hath not God. He that abideth in the doctrine of Christ, he hath both the Father and the Son. If there come any unto you, and bring not this doctrine, receive him not into your house, neither bid him

God speed: *For he that biddeth him God speed is partaker of his evil deeds"* (II John 7—11).

"Those things which we have WROUGHT" speaks of stewardship—*works,* not salvation. Certainly we have not "wrought" our salvation, for the Lamb of God purchased salvation through the sacrifice of Himself on the cross. John is warning us in this passage that if we give support, comfort, or encouragement to the enemies of our Lord we will lose part of our reward—perhaps *ALL of it.* Believers should be careful about lending either their presence or their financial support to a church where the Gospel is not preached in all of its purity and power. God's Word says *"we must ALL appear before the judgment seat of Christ,"* and that means not one believer will be excused, each and every one *must* appear to give an account of deeds done in the body.

I would emphasize, however, that *this is NOT judgment for sin.* It is the judgment *for believers only,* and only works and stewardship will be judged. Our salvation and eternal destiny are determined in this life, and if we are *not* saved in this life we certainly will not be saved in the life to come! No *unsaved* person will appear before the judgment seat of Christ. The unsaved dead will not be raised until a thousand years after the resurrection of the righteous, and the unsaved at the time of the Rapture will not be changed as the righteous will be changed. Revelation 20:4—6 tells us that the saints of God will live and reign with Christ for a thousand years, *"but the rest of the dead* (the wicked dead) *lived not again until the thousand years were finished. This is the first resurrection.* Blessed and holy is he that hath part in the first resurrection: on such the second death hath no power, but they shall be priests of God and of Christ, *and*

133

shall reign with Him a thousand years."

The salvation of believers is settled when they believe on the Lord Jesus Christ and accept His finished work, and *there is "NO CONDEMNATION to them which are in Christ Jesus"* (Rom. 8:1). Christ Himself declared that all who believe on Him *HAVE EVERLASTING LIFE and shall not come into condemnation*—or judgment (John 5:24).

It is the *service* of believers, not their salvation, that will be dealt with at the judgment seat of Christ. In I Corinthians 4:5 the Apostle Paul admonishes, "Therefore judge nothing before the time, until the Lord come, who both will *bring to light the hidden things of darkness,* and will *make manifest the counsels of the hearts:* and then shall every man have praise of God."

Hear this, beloved: Before the judgment seat of Christ, *all hidden secrets* will be uncovered, and *unconfessed sins* in the believer's life will be brought to light! Our *works* will be made manifest, they will be revealed "by fire"—that is, by the Word of God—for His Word is "like as a fire . . . and like a hammer that breaketh the rock in pieces" (Jer. 23:29). Our works will be tried by fire, and those whose works stand the fire-test will receive a reward. Those whose works are *burned* will suffer loss—but they will not suffer damnation in hell. This is Gospel truth just as surely as John 3:16 is Gospel truth. John the Beloved urges us, "Little children, abide in Him; that, when He shall appear, we may have confidence, and not be *ashamed before Him* at His coming" (I John 2:28).

Believers who live according to the Word of God, faithfully serving Him with heart, mind, and strength, will receive a reward. We are not told just what these rewards will be, this is one of the "secret things" that belong unto the Lord (Deut. 29:29); but we may rest assured that the rewards we receive will be as glorious as the Christ who saved us. He could do no less!

Then when the judgment seat of Christ is past, He will lead His saints into the Father's house and we will behold the glory of God the Father. This was included in the Saviour's prayer of intercession: "Father, I will that they also, whom thou hast given me, be with me where I am; that they may behold my glory, which thou hast given me: for thou lovedst me before the foundation of the world" (John 17:24).

It is then that Christ will present the Church to Himself—"a glorious Church, not having spot, or wrinkle, or any such thing . . . holy and without blemish" (Eph. 5:27). He will present His Church "faultless before the presence of His glory with exceeding joy" (Jude 24).

The Crowning Day—Five Crowns

The New Testament speaks of five crowns which may be earned by believers:

The Crown of Life:—

"Blessed is the man that endureth temptation: for when he is tried, *he shall receive THE CROWN OF LIFE,* which the Lord hath promised to them that love Him" (James 1:12).

"Fear none of those things which thou shalt suffer: behold, the devil shall cast some of you into prison, that ye may be tried; and ye shall have tribulation ten days: be thou faithful unto death, and *I will give thee A CROWN OF LIFE*" (Rev. 2:10).

Not every believer will earn the crown of life. It is

135

the martyr's crown and it will be given only to those who are martyred for their testimony. The passage just given from Revelation refers primarily to the saints who will be martyred during the tribulation period.

The Crown of Glory: —

"Feed the flock of God which is among you, taking the oversight thereof, not by constraint, but willingly; not for filthy lucre, but of a ready mind; neither as being lords over God's heritage, but being ensamples to the flock. And when the Chief Shepherd shall appear, *ye shall receive A CROWN OF GLORY that fadeth not away*" (I Pet. 5:2—4).

This is *the pastor's crown,* and when Jesus, the Chief Shepherd, shall appear He will give this crown to God's ministers who have been faithful undershepherds, feeding the flock to the glory of God and "not for filthy lucre." God's men are to serve where He puts them—not as "lords over God's heritage," but as an example to the flock.

The Crown of Rejoicing: —

"*What is our hope, or joy, or CROWN OF RE-JOICING?* Are not even ye in the presence of our Lord Jesus Christ at His coming? For *ye are our glory and joy*" (I Thess. 2:19, 20).

"Therefore, my brethren dearly beloved and longed for, *my joy and CROWN,* so stand fast in the Lord, my beloved" (Phil. 4:1).

The *crown of rejoicing* is *the soul-winner's crown.* It can—and should—be earned by every born again believer. It is true that not all believers are *full time* soul-winners, but certainly all believers can let their light shine when and where they come in contact with those who are lost in the darkness of sin. There are so many places, so many opportunities, to point men to Christ.

The Crown of Righteousness:—

"Henceforth there is laid up for me *a crown of righteousness*, which the Lord, the righteous Judge, shall give me at that day: and not to me only, but *unto them also that LOVE HIS APPEARING*" (II Tim. 4:8).

The crown of righteousness will be given to those who "love His appearing"—i. e., those who long for and pray for the second coming of Jesus. Our Bible closes with such a prayer—"Even so, *COME, Lord Jesus*" (Rev. 22:20). We should be so in love with Jesus that we would pray daily for His soon return, and all who love His appearing will receive a crown of righteousness.

The Incorruptible Crown:—

"And every man that *striveth for the mastery* is temperate in all things. Now they do it to obtain a corruptible crown; *but we an INCORRUPTIBLE*" (I Cor. 9:25).

"And now, little children, abide in Him; that, when He shall appear, we may have confidence, and not be ashamed before Him at His coming" (I John 2:28).

This is *the victor's crown,* and it will be given to those who are victorious over the world, the flesh, and the devil—those who do not permit themselves to be diverted from the Master's work by yielding to fleshly lusts and indulging in worldly amusements and worldly pleasures. If we do not want to be "ashamed at His coming" let us so live that the flesh with its appetites and affections will be kept in subjection, so that whatever we do may be done to the

137

glory of God.

Christ's Future Work In Connection With the Earth: The Tribulation Period

"And I saw in the right hand of Him that sat on the throne a book written within and on the backside, sealed with seven seals. And I saw a strong angel proclaiming with a loud voice, Who is worthy to open the book, and to loose the seals thereof? And no man in heaven, nor in earth, neither under the earth, was able to open the book, neither to look thereon. And I wept much, because no man was found worthy to open and to read the book, neither to look thereon.

"And one of the elders saith unto me, Weep not: behold, the Lion of the tribe of Juda, the Root of David, hath prevailed to open the book, and to loose the seven seals thereof. And I beheld, and, lo, in the midst of the throne and of the four beasts, and in the midst of the elders, stood a Lamb as it had been slain, having seven horns and seven eyes, which are the seven Spirits of God sent forth into all the earth. And He came and took the book out of the right hand of Him that sat upon the throne.

"And when He had taken the book, the four beasts and four and twenty elders fell down before the Lamb, having every one of them harps, and golden vials full of odours, which are the prayers of saints. And they sung a new song, saying, Thou art worthy to take the book, and to open the seals thereof: for thou wast slain, and hast redeemed us to God by thy blood out of every kindred, and tongue, and people, and nation; and hast made us unto our God kings and priests: and we shall reign on the earth.

"And I beheld, and I heard the voice of many angels round about the throne and the beasts and the elders: and the number of them was ten thousand times ten thousand, and thousands of thousands; saying with a loud voice, *Worthy is the Lamb that was slain to receive power, and riches, and*

wisdom, and strength, and honour, and glory, and blessing.
And every creature which is in heaven, and on the earth, and
under the earth, and such as are in the sea, and all that are
in them, heard I saying, *Blessing, and honour, and glory, and
power, be unto Him that sitteth upon the throne, and unto
the Lamb for ever and ever.*

"And the four beasts said, *Amen.* And the four and twenty
elders *fell down and worshipped Him that liveth for ever and
ever"* (Rev. 5:1—14).

When the saints of God are caught up to meet the
Lord in the air and when events previously discussed
have taken place, the Lord Jesus Christ will then begin
from heaven a work which will be severely felt throughout the whole earth. After believers appear before the
judgment seat of Christ and have been rewarded for
faithful stewardship, we will crown Him *Lord of all.*
He will then begin to deal with the world in a series
of judgments that are clearly outlined in the book of
Revelation—and in other parts of both the Old and
New Testaments.

*"I saw in the right hand of Him that sat on the
throne A BOOK . . . ."* This little book contains the
terms of the redemption of the earth. Today—and
every day since Adam sinned—the whole creation
groans and travails in pain; but one day Christ will
deliver this earth from the curse. The book received
by the Lamb contains the *judgments* decreed to take
place on earth, with its apostate masses of humanity.
The Lamb of God is seen opening the seven seals of
the book, and as He breaks the seals the events described under each of the seven seals occur. This is
Christ's work in judgment.

"And when He had opened the seventh seal, there
was silence in heaven about the space of half an hour.
And I saw the seven angels which stood before God;

and to them were given seven trumpets. And another Angel came and stood at the altar, having a golden censer: and there was given unto Him much incense, that He should offer it with the prayers of all saints upon the golden altar which was before the throne. And the smoke of the incense, which came with the prayers of the saints, ascended up before God out of the Angel's hand. And the Angel took the censer, and filled it with fire of the altar, and cast it into the earth: and there were voices, and thunderings, and lightnings, and an earthquake. *And the seven angels which had the seven trumpets prepared themselves to sound"* (Rev. 8:1—6).

In this passage, the Angel standing before the altar is none other than the Lord Jesus Christ, and He casts down the fire of divine displeasure and divine judgment upon this earth. It is He who sends forth the seven angels with trumpets. Then in Revelation chapters 15 and 16 we see seven other angels, each holding a vial filled with the wrath of Almighty God. It would take entirely too much time and space to discuss each of these judgments separately and at length, but we will mention briefly what occurs when the seven trumpets sound:

"When He had opened the seventh seal, *there was silence in heaven about the space of half an hour."* There is but one explanation for the statement recorded here: When the seventh seal is removed from the little book, the thing that occurs is so horrible that all heaven stands aghast and all activity ceases for about half an hour. Then the seven trumpets begin to sound, each in turn.

As the *first angel* sounded his trumpet, "there followed hail and fire mingled with blood, and they were cast upon the earth: and the third part of trees was

140

burnt up, and all green grass was burnt up."

Then the *second angel* sounded—"and as it were a great mountain burning with fire was cast into the sea: and the third part of the sea became blood; and the third part of the creatures which were in the sea, and had life, died; and the third part of the ships were destroyed."

After this, the *third angel* sounded his trumpet, "and there fell a great star from heaven, burning as it were a lamp, and it fell upon the third part of the rivers, and upon the fountains of waters: And the name of the star is called Wormwood: and the third part of the waters became wormwood; and many men died of the waters, because they were made bitter."

Then the *fourth angel* sounded, "and the third part of the sun was smitten, and the third part of the moon, and the third part of the stars; so as the third part of them was darkened, and the day shone not for a third part of it, and the night likewise. And I beheld, and heard an angel flying through the midst of heaven, saying with a loud voice, *Woe, woe, woe, to the inhabiters of the earth* by reason of the other voices of the trumpet of the three angels, *which are yet to sound!*" (Rev. 8:7—13).

After the woes are pronounced, the *fifth angel* sounded his trumpet and John saw a star (the Lord Jesus Christ) fall from heaven, "and to Him was given the key of the bottomless pit. And He opened the bottomless pit; and there arose a smoke out of the pit, as the smoke of a great furnace; and the sun and the air were darkened by reason of the smoke of the pit. And there came out of the smoke locusts upon the earth: and unto them was given power, as the scorpions of the earth have power."

These locusts will be given power to torment men

for five months (except for those who have the seal of God in their foreheads), and the torment will be so unbearable that men will beg for death but cannot die! These demon monstrosities are described in detail in Revelation 9:7−11. This is the first of the three woes pronounced by the angel in Revelation 8:13, and there are yet two woes to follow.

The *sixth angel* now sounds his trumpet, and four angels are loosed from the great river Euphrates, each of them prepared for battle "for to slay the third part of men. And the number of the army of the horsemen were two hundred thousand thousand: and I heard the number of them. And thus I saw the horses in the vision, and them that sat on them, having breast-plates of fire, and of jacinth, and brimstone: and the heads of the horses were as the heads of lions; and out of their mouths issued fire and smoke and brimstone. By these three was the third part of men killed: by the *fire,* and by the *smoke,* and by the *brimstone,* which issued out of their mouths" (Rev. 9:13−18). But even then, the remainder of the people on earth *"repented not"!*

In chapter 10 of Revelation we are told of the mighty Angel and the little book. This mighty Angel of course is none other than the Lord Jesus Christ, and "He had in His hand a little book open." The Son of God in angelic form now placed His left foot upon the land and His right foot upon the sea, "and cried with a loud voice, as when a lion roareth"—yes, *the Lion of the tribe of Judah!* "And when He had cried, seven thunders uttered their voices." John was about to write what the seven thunders said, but a voice from heaven instructed him to *"seal up* those things which the seven thunders uttered, *and write them not."*

Then the mighty Angel lifted His hand to heaven and swore that time should be no more, "but in the days of the voice of the seventh angel, when he shall begin to sound, the mystery of God should be finished, *as He hath declared to His servants the prophets*" (Rev. 10:1—7). In the remaining verses of chapter 10 John is instructed to take the little book and eat it. He finds it sweet in his mouth but bitter in the inner man.

Revelation 11:1—14 records "the times of the Gentiles," the three and one-half years of severe tribulation. As yet, the seventh trumpet has not sounded, but now the trumpet judgments are resumed and the *seventh angel* sounds his trumpet—"and there were great voices in heaven, saying, The kingdoms of this world are become the kingdoms of our Lord, and of His Christ; and He shall reign for ever and ever. And the four and twenty elders, which sat before God on their seats, fell upon their faces, and worshipped God" (Rev. 11:15, 16).

In Revelation 15:1 John "saw another sign in heaven, great and marvellous—seven angels having the seven last plagues; for *in them is filled up the wrath of God!*" Moving on into Revelation chapter 16 we see these seven vials of wrath poured upon the earth— yes, this same earth where we live today.

In Revelation 16:1 John "heard a great voice out of the temple," instructing the seven angels, "Go your ways, and pour out the vials of the wrath of God!" The seven angels were to go their separate ways, and they were to *pour out*—not just part of the wrath of God, but they were to empty the vials unto the last bitter dreg! Each angel had his individual instructions.

The *first vial* was poured out upon the *earth*, "and

there fell *a noisome and grievous sore* upon the men which had the mark of the beast, and upon them which worshipped his image."

The *second vial* was poured out upon the *sea*—"and it became as the blood of a dead man: and every living soul died in the sea!" What a terrible stench will one day engulf this world!

The *third vial* was poured out "upon *the rivers and fountains of waters;* and they became blood."

The *fourth vial* was poured out upon the *sun,* "and power was given unto him to scorch men with fire. And men were scorched with great heat, and blasphemed the name of God, which hath power over these plagues: *and they REPENTED NOT to give Him glory.*"

The *fifth vial* was poured out upon the seat of the *beast,* "and his kingdom was full of darkness. (Men) gnawed their tongues for pain, and blasphemed the God of heaven because of their pains and their sores, *and REPENTED NOT of their deeds.*"

The *sixth vial* was poured out upon *the great river Euphrates*—"and the water thereof was dried up, that the way of the kings of the east might be prepared." The river Euphrates will be dried up and a great highway will be prepared for the kings of the east to make ready for the last gigantic blood bath. Notice John saw *"three unclean spirits* like frogs come out of the mouth of the dragon, and out of the mouth of the beast, and out of the mouth of the false prophet." This is the Satanic trinity. They will be evil spirits, spirits of devils, working great miracles—and please notice they go forth to *the whole world,* "to gather them to the battle of that great day of God Almighty" (Rev. 16:12—14).

This gathering will be in the Valley of Armageddon

just outside Jerusalem, and it is then that Jesus will come and destroy these great armies (which will be led by the devil himself). At that time there will be such a blood-bath as this world has never known, and God's Word tells us that blood will flow *"even unto the horse bridles"* for a thousand and six hundred furlongs—(or a distance of two hundred miles)! (Read Revelation 14:14—20.)

Then John saw the *seventh vial* of God's wrath being poured out:

"And the seventh angel poured out his vial into *the air:* and there came *a great voice out of the temple of heaven, from the throne, saying, IT IS DONE!* And there were voices, and thunders, and lightnings; and there was a great earthquake, such as was not since men were upon the earth, so mighty an earthquake, and so great. And the great city was divided into three parts, and the cities of the nations fell: and great Babylon came in remembrance before God, to give unto her the cup of the wine of the fierceness of His wrath. And every island fled away, and the mountains were not found. *And there fell upon men a great hail out of heaven, every stone about the weight of a talent: and men blasphemed God because of the plague of the hail; for the plague thereof was exceeding great"* (Rev. 16:17—21).

"IT IS DONE!" Hallelujah! When Jesus paid the supreme price for the redemption of sinners, He cried out from the cross, *"It is finished!"* Redemption for the soul is complete in Jesus—and now the judgment of the earth, too, is finished. Jesus Christ will now rid the earth of the dragon, the beast, and the false prophet. The contents of the little seven-sealed book are completed, every minute detail has been carried out, and the whole creation at last will cease to groan

and travail in pain (Rom. 8:22).

But the severity of the judgment of this seventh vial of the wrath of God will be without parallel in human history. The air will go into mighty convulsions, there will be lightnings, thunderings, and voices. From the sky will fall hailstones "about the weight of a *talent.*" At the time of the writing of the book of Revelation, talents varied in weight. The Jewish talent of silver was 115 pounds. An Egyptian talent was 86 pounds. In Antioch talents of 390 pounds were used. So whatever the weight of the "talent" in our present Scripture, the hailstones here described will be beyond anything this world has ever known. Imagine the chaos that will come about on earth when chunks of ice weighing from one to three hundred pounds begin to fall from heaven. Yet we note again, *"Men blasphemed God* because of the plague of the hail."

Do I believe these judgments will occur literally? Indeed I do! This is part of the future work of our Lord and Saviour, Jesus Christ, and I believe it will occur just as it is laid down in God's Word. I see no reason to spiritualize these judgments. God's Word cannot fail, and since all other prophecies have been fulfilled pertaining to the birth, death, resurrection, and return to glory of our Lord, I believe these judgments will take place exactly as they are prophesied— from the removing of the first seal in Revelation 6:1 to the pouring out of the seventh vial of God's wrath, and the great cry from the throne of God, "IT IS DONE!"

Who Will Go Through These Horrible Judgments?

When the Rapture occurs, all born again believers and innocent children will be taken out of this world, caught up to meet Jesus in the air. There will be not one born again person left upon the face of the earth! Those who will go through the Great Tribulation will be *apostate mankind.*

Israel as a nation back in their own land will pass through those judgments executed from heaven by the Lamb of God Himself. God-defying, Christ-rejecting Christendom (the Laodiceans who will be "spued out") will enter the tribulation—*and most of them will DIE before it is over!* However, instead of causing men to repent, these horrible judgments will cause them to *blaspheme God.* They will have the same spirit Pharaoh had when his heart was hardened and he refused to let the children of Israel leave Egypt.

The people on earth at the time of the tribulation will believe "strong delusions" and will accept and worship the Man of Sin because of his lying wonders and the great miracles he will perform. He will sit in the temple, announcing that he is God, and the masses of humanity will *follow* him as God.

The Great Tribulation will center in and around Jerusalem, but it will extend to the ends of the earth. The apostate Jews will worship the Antichrist, they will literally bow down to him and worship him as their forefathers worshipped Jehovah God. But there will be *a small remnant* of God-fearing Jews who will refuse to bow down to the Man of Sin, just as there is a remnant of Jews today who have placed their trust in the Lord Jesus Christ and are looking forward to the time when as King He will reign from the throne of David in Jerusalem. However, believing Jews (those who are saved *during* the tribulation period) will suffer terrible persecution. Most of them will be put to death.

Jewish believers will be *the last messengers of the*

King just before He comes to occupy the throne of David. They will preach the Gospel of the kingdom to the ends of the earth, to the multi-millions who will not be reached by the Church with the Gospel of grace. They will once more herald the good news of their soon-coming King, and before the end of time they will bear witness to all nations around the earth. Jesus said, "This Gospel of the kingdom shall be preached in all the world for a witness unto all nations; and then shall the end come" (Matt. 24:14).

There are teachings in this land today which declare that God is finished with the Jews and that all of the promises to Abraham will be fulfilled in the Church. This is error, it is wrongly dividing the Word of God. God *has not* forgotten Israel, He will *never* forget that nation; and one day He will again visit them and the Jews as a nation will be saved. This is clearly set forth in Paul's letter to the believers at Rome:

"I say then, *Hath God cast away His people?* God forbid! For I also am an Israelite, of the seed of Abraham, of the tribe of Benjamin. *GOD HATH NOT CAST AWAY HIS PEOPLE WHICH HE FOREKNEW.* Wot ye not what the Scripture saith of Elias? how he maketh intercession to God against Israel, saying, *Lord, they have killed thy prophets, and digged down thine altars; and I am left alone, and they seek my life.*

"But what saith the answer of God unto him? *I have reserved to myself SEVEN THOUSAND MEN, who have not bowed the knee to the image of Baal.*

"Even so then *at this present time also* there is a remnant according to the election of grace. And if by grace, then is it no more of works: otherwise grace is no more grace. But if it be of works, then is it no more grace: otherwise work is no more work.

Future: The Tribulation Period

"What then? Israel hath not obtained that which he seeketh for; but the election hath obtained it, *and the rest were blinded* (according as it is written, God hath given them the spirit of slumber, eyes that they should not see, and ears that they should not hear) *unto this day.*

"And David saith, Let their table be made a snare, and a trap, and a stumblingblock, and a recompence unto them: Let their eyes be darkened, that they may not see, and bow down their back alway.

"I say then, *Have they stumbled that they should fall?* God forbid! But rather through their fall salvation is come unto the Gentiles, for to provoke them to jealousy. Now if the fall of them be the riches of the world, and the diminishing of them the riches of the Gentiles; *how much more their fulness?* For I speak to you Gentiles, inasmuch as I am the apostle of the Gentiles, I magnify mine office: if by any means I may provoke to emulation them which are my flesh, and might save some of them. For if the *casting away of them* be the reconciling of the world, *what shall the receiving of them be,* but life from the dead? For if the firstfruit be holy, the lump is also holy: and if the root be holy, so are the branches. And if some of the branches be broken off, and thou, being a wild olive tree, wert graffed in among them, and with them partakest of the root and fatness of the olive tree; boast not against the branches. But if thou boast, thou bearest not the root, but the root thee.

"Thou wilt say then, The branches were broken off, that I might be graffed in. Well; *because of UNBELIEF they were broken off,* and thou standest by faith. Be not highminded, but fear: for if God spared not the *natural* branches, take heed lest He also spare not *thee.*

"Behold therefore the goodness and severity of God: on them which fell, severity; but toward thee, goodness, if thou continue in His goodness: otherwise thou also shalt be cut off. *And they also, if they abide not still in unbelief, shall be graffed in:* for God is able to graff them in again. For if thou wert cut out of the olive tree which is wild by nature, and wert graffed contrary to nature into a good olive tree: how much more shall these, which be the *natural* branches, be graffed into their own olive tree?

"For I would not, brethren, that ye should be ignorant of this mystery, lest ye should be wise in your own conceits; that *blindness IN PART is happened to Israel, until the fulness of the Gentiles be come in. And so ALL ISRAEL SHALL BE SAVED. As it is written, There shall come out of Sion the Deliverer, and shall turn away ungodliness from Jacob: for this is my covenant unto them, when I shall TAKE AWAY THEIR SINS.*

"As concerning the Gospel, they are enemies for your sakes: but as touching the election, they are beloved for the fathers' sakes. *For the gifts and calling of God are without repentance.* For as ye in times past have not believed God, yet have now obtained mercy through their unbelief: even so have these also now not believed, that through your mercy they also may obtain mercy. For God hath concluded them all in unbelief, that He might have mercy upon all.

"O the depth of the riches both of the wisdom and knowledge of God! how unsearchable are His judgments, and His ways past finding out! For who hath known the mind of the Lord? or who hath been His counsellor? Or who hath first given to Him, and it shall be recompensed unto him again? For of Him, and through Him, and to Him, are all things: to whom be glory for ever. Amen" (Rom. 11:1—36).

The Future Work of Christ and the Nations

"In that day shall this song be sung in the land of Judah: We have a strong city; salvation will God appoint for walls and bulwarks. Open ye the gates, that the righteous nation which keepeth the truth may enter in. Thou wilt keep him in perfect peace, whose mind is stayed on thee: because he trusteth in thee.

"Trust ye in the Lord for ever: for in the Lord JEHOVAH is everlasting strength: For He bringeth down them that dwell on high; the lofty city, He layeth it low; He layeth it low, even to the ground: He bringeth it even to the dust. The foot shall tread it down, even the feet of the poor, and the steps of the needy.

"The way of the just is uprightness: thou, most upright, dost weigh the path of the just. Yea, in the way of thy judgments, O Lord, have we waited for thee; the desire of our soul is to thy name, and to the remembrance of thee. With my soul have I desired thee in the night; yea, with my spirit within me will I seek thee early: *for WHEN THY JUDG-MENTS ARE IN THE EARTH, the inhabitants of the world will learn righteousness"* (Isa. 26:1–9).

Here we see the worship and testimony of Israel *converted and restored.* "When thy judgments are in the earth" speaks of the horrible judgments which will be poured out upon the earth at the end of the Great Tribulation. Israel will be severely judged— but out of the judgment they will come forth *converted as a nation.* When Israel is converted, they will return to the Lord their God, and the nations of the world "will learn righteousness"—that is, they will seek the Lord because of the exceeding blessings of Jehovah upon Israel, and Jerusalem will be the capital city of the world.

During the seven years of tribulation the work of salvation will go on. Revelation 7:1–8 tells us that 144,000 Jewish missionaries will be sealed for God's service—12,000 from each of the twelve tribes of Israel—and during the tribulation period these men will preach the Gospel of the kingdom to every creature on the face of this earth. Not all persons who hear that Gospel will be saved, but there will be *a great multitude* saved and they will seal their testimony with their life's blood:

"After this (after the sealing of the 144,000) I beheld, and, lo, *a great multitude, which no man could number, of all nations, and kindreds, and people, and tongues, stood before the throne, and before the Lamb, clothed in white robes, and palms in their hands; and cried with a loud voice, saying, Salvation to our God which sitteth upon the throne, and unto the Lamb.* And all the angels stood round about the throne, and about the elders and the four beasts, and fell before the throne on their faces, and worshipped God, saying, Amen: Blessing, and glory, and wisdom, and thanksgiving, and honour, and power, and might, be unto our God for ever and ever. Amen.

"And one of the elders answered, saying unto me, *What are these which are arrayed in white robes? and whence came they?* And I said unto him, Sir, thou knowest. And he said to me, *These are they which came out of GREAT TRIBULATION, and have washed their robes, and made them white IN THE BLOOD OF THE LAMB. Therefore are they before the throne of God, and serve Him day and night in His temple: and He that sitteth on the throne shall dwell among them. They shall hunger no more, neither thirst any more; neither shall the sun light on them, nor any heat. For the Lamb which is in the midst of the throne shall feed them, and shall lead them unto living fountains of waters: and GOD SHALL WIPE AWAY ALL TEARS FROM THEIR EYES"* (Rev. 7:9—17).

Although heathen nations will hear and accept the Gospel, apostate Christendom will be excluded because they will have *heard* the truth and rejected it before the Rapture. Paul explains this in II Thessalonians 2:1—12:

152

Future: Christ and the Nations

"Now we beseech you, brethren, by the coming of our Lord Jesus Christ, and by our gathering together unto Him, that ye be not soon shaken in mind, or be troubled, neither by spirit, nor by word, nor by letter as from us, as that the day of Christ is at hand. Let no man deceive you by any means: for that day shall not come, except there come a falling away first, and that Man of Sin be revealed, the son of perdition; who opposeth and exalteth himself above all that is called God, or that is worshipped; so that he as God sitteth in the temple of God, shewing himself that he is God.

"Remember ye not, that, when I was yet with you, I told you these things? And now ye know what withholdeth that he might be revealed in his time. For the mystery of iniquity doth already work: only He (the Holy Spirit) who now letteth will let, until He be taken out of the way. And then shall that Wicked be revealed, whom the Lord shall consume with the spirit of His mouth, and shall destroy with the brightness of His coming: even Him, whose coming is after the working of Satan with all power and signs and lying wonders, and with all deceivableness of unrighteousness in them that perish; *because they received not the love of the truth, that they might be saved.*

"And for this cause GOD SHALL SEND THEM STRONG DELUSION, that they should believe a lie: that they all might be damned who BELIEVED NOT THE TRUTH, but had pleasure in unrighteousness."

In Revelation chapter 21, John the Beloved describes the New Jerusalem, the Pearly White City which will be the home of the New Testament Church, the bride of Christ. Following that description, he declares, "The city had no need of the sun, neither of the moon, to shine in it: for the glory of God did lighten it, and the Lamb is the light thereof. *And the NA-TIONS of them which are SAVED shall walk in the light of it . . ."* (Rev. 21:23, 24). These saved nations are the nations which will refuse to follow Gog and Magog after the Millennium.

The Revelation of Jesus Christ

The second coming of Christ will be in two stages: *the Rapture* (when He will descend in the air and call the Church up to meet Him) and *the Revelation* (approximately seven years after the Rapture when He will stand on the Mount of Olives and every eye shall see Him). We have already discussed the Rapture, the first phase of His second coming. Now let us look at some of the Scriptures which describe His appearing in the Revelation.

In Matthew 24:29—31 Jesus said, "Immediately after the tribulation of those days shall the sun be darkened, and the moon shall not give her light, and the stars shall fall from heaven, and the powers of the heavens shall be shaken: and then shall appear the sign of the Son of man in heaven: and then shall all the tribes of the earth mourn, and *they shall see the Son of man coming in the clouds of heaven WITH POWER AND GREAT GLORY*. And He shall send His angels with a great sound of a trumpet, and they shall gather together His elect from the four winds, from one end of heaven to the other."

This is definitely the Revelation, not the Rapture. When Christ comes in the first phase of His second appearing He will not be seen or heard by any but the saints, the believers, nor will there be any outstanding signs in the heavens as we note here—the darkening of the sun, the moon giving forth no light, the stars falling from heaven. Then notice "all tribes of the earth" will *see* the Son of man, He will come "with power and great glory," and all tribes of the earth will mourn.

154

The same appearing is described in Revelation 1:7: "Behold, He cometh with clouds; and *every eye shall see Him,* and they also which pierced Him: and *all kindreds of the earth shall wail because of Him.* Even so, Amen."

This phase of Christ's second coming is also described in Revelation 6:12—17 where the sixth seal is broken:

"And I beheld when He had opened the sixth seal, and, lo, there was a great earthquake; and the sun became black as sackcloth of hair, and the moon became as blood; and the stars of heaven fell unto the earth, even as a fig tree casteth her untimely figs, when she is shaken of a mighty wind. And the heaven departed as a scroll when it is rolled together; and every mountain and island were moved out of their places.

"And the kings of the earth, and the great men, and the rich men, and the chief captains, and the mighty men, and every bondman, and every free man, hid themselves in the dens and in the rocks of the mountains; and said to the mountains and rocks, *Fall on us, and hide us from the face of Him that sitteth on the throne, and from the wrath of the Lamb: for THE GREAT DAY OF HIS WRATH IS COME; and who shall be able to stand?"*

What a terrible day this will be for those who have served the Antichrist! They will beg for the mountains and rocks to fall on them, that they may be hidden from the face of Him who sits on the throne. They will try to hide in "the dens and rocks of the mountains" in order to escape the wrath of the Lamb of God. A great earthquake will shake this earth, the sun will be *black* in its darkness and the moon will become as blood! The stars of heaven will fall from their places and the heavens will be rolled together like a scroll. The mountains and islands of the earth will be moved out of their accustomed places. Yes, beloved, I believe this is *a literal description* of the time when Christ will come in glory, when every person on earth will see Him and will try to hide from Him to escape His mighty wrath!

Revelation 19:11−16 describes this same event: "I saw heaven opened, and behold a white horse; and He that sat upon him was called Faithful and True, and in righteousness He doth judge and make war. His eyes were as a flame of fire, and on His head were many crowns; and He had a name written, that no man knew, but He Himself. And He was clothed with a vesture dipped in blood: and His name is called The Word of God.

"And the armies which were in heaven followed Him upon white horses, clothed in fine linen, white and clean. And out of His mouth goeth a sharp sword, that with it He should smite the nations: and He shall rule them with a rod of iron, and He treadeth the winepress of the fierceness and wrath of Almighty God. And He hath on His vesture and on His thigh a name written, KING OF KINGS, AND LORD OF LORDS!"

There can be no question as to the identity of this Person. "His name is called *the Word of God,*" and the Word of God is Jesus (John 1:1, 14). His eyes are as flaming fire and He wears many crowns on His head—this occurs after we crown Him King of kings and Lord of lords. He is called *Faithful and True,* and "in righteousness He doth judge and make war." In other words, His actions are righteous, and only the Lord Jesus Christ could fit that description. We see Him here as the mighty Warrior-King, victorious

156

in battle, conquering in righteous power. This is not a war for the love of conquest or to enlarge a king's dominion, but to put down evil and enthrone righteousness on earth. He is clothed *with a vesture dipped in blood*—not His own blood, but the blood of His enemies. He comes now to deal with the opposing armies of Antichrist, armies gathered together in war against the Lamb.

The armies of heaven are the saints of God, riding on white horses and clothed in white linen. The *"sharp sword"* with which He will smite the nations is the Word of God—described in Hebrews 4:12 as "quick and powerful . . . sharper than any twoedged sword, piercing even to the dividing asunder of soul and spirit, and of the joints and marrow, and is a discerner of the thoughts and intents of the heart." The name written "on His vesture and on His thigh" announces Him as *KING OF KINGS, and LORD OF LORDS*. Yes, this Person can be none other than the Lord Jesus Christ, coming not as the Lamb of God, meek and lowly, but as the King of heaven and earth, in might and royal majesty, with millions of shining angels with Him. His glory will cover the heavens, and the earth will be full of His praise (Hab. 3:3).

His visible and glorious coming will be the crowning and unanswerable proof of His deity, and every denying tongue since Adam will be forever hushed! Every unbeliever—from those who cried, "Crucify Him!" to those who will be living at His coming—will be forced to confess that He is God's Christ. ". . . Every knee shall bow . . . and every tongue shall confess to God" (Rom. 14:11). In that glorious day of victory and triumph "He shall come to be glorified in His saints and to be admired in all them that

157

believe . . ." (II Thess. 1:10).

Christ's Judgment Work

"Behold, the day of the Lord cometh, and thy spoil shall be divided in the midst of thee. For I will gather all nations against Jerusalem to battle; and the city shall be taken, and the houses rifled, and the women ravished; and half of the city shall go forth into captivity, and the residue of the people shall not be cut off from the city. Then shall the Lord go forth, and fight against those nations, as when He fought in the day of battle" (Zech. 14:1—3).

When Jesus comes as King of kings and Lord of lords, He will judge the wicked. His feet will stand once more upon the Mount of Olives, and before the city of Jerusalem all nations will be gathered to do battle in Satan's last great drive to destroy the holy city. The beast will be the commander-in-chief of the army, and the Man of Sin will do his dreadful work in the city of Jerusalem itself.

The remnant of the nation of Israel, in great distress, will then pray to Jehovah God for deliverance, they will look to Him to bring victory and peace, and their deliverance will come with the coming of their King. They will shout for joy and will cry out, "Lo, this is our God! We have waited for Him, and He will save us. This is the Lord! We have waited for Him, we will be glad and rejoice in His salvation" (Isa. 25:9).

It is then that the great and terrible battle of Armageddon will take place. The kings of earth and the armies of earth will gather around the holy city Jerusalem and will declare war against the Christ and His armies (Rev. 19:19). But the battle will come to a sudden end, the opposition will be suddenly broken:

"And the beast was taken, and with him the false prophet that wrought miracles before him, with which he deceived them that had received the mark of the beast, and them that worshipped his image. *These both were cast alive into a lake of fire burning with brimstone. And the remnant were slain with the sword of Him that sat upon the horse, which sword proceeded out of His mouth: and all the fowls were filled with their flesh*" (Rev. 19:20, 21).

The pride of the armies of the Antichrist will lie in the dust of the earth in death—not killed with bullets or atomic bombs, but with the sword that proceeds out of the mouth of the King of kings! The voice of His fury will strike suddenly, taking the lives of chiefs, captains, kings—and their flesh will be devoured by the fowls of the air. And the beast and the false prophet will be cast alive into the lake of fire—yes, *literal fire*, the fire of hell, "where their worm dieth not, and the fire is not quenched" (Mark 9:43–48).

The Judgments

There is no such thing as a "general resurrection" or a "general judgment," and those who teach such doctrine are wrongly dividing the Word of God. The Scripture clearly speaks of five separate judgments and three thrones. The *thrones* are mentioned as "the judgment seat of Christ" (II Cor. 5:10); "the throne of His glory" (Matt. 25:31, 32); and "the Great White Throne" (Rev. 20:11, 12).

The judgments also differ—in five different aspects: (1) subject; (2) time; (3) place; (4) basis; (5) result. We will consider each of these judgments in turn:

Judgment Number One:—
"(Christ) His own self *bare our sins in His own*

body on the tree, that we, being *dead to sins,* should live unto righteousness: by whose stripes ye were healed" (I Pet. 2:24).

"For Christ also hath once *suffered for SINS,* the Just for the unjust, *that He might bring us to God,* being put to death in the flesh, but quickened by the Spirit" (I Pet. 3:18).

"Christ hath redeemed us from the curse of the law, being made a curse for us: for it is written, Cursed is every one that hangeth on a tree" (Gal. 3:13).

"There is therefore now *NO CONDEMNATION to them which are in Christ Jesus,* who walk not after the flesh, but after the Spirit" (Rom. 8:1).

The *subjects* of this judgment are believers as having to do with sin. Jesus judged sin for us when He died on the cross.

The *time* of this judgment was about 30 A. D., and the *place* where it occurred was Calvary.

The *basis* of this judgment is Christ's finished work, and the *result* of the judgment is *justification of all who believe in His finished work.*

This judgment is past. It occurred almost two thousand years ago when Jesus died on the cross. Notice: He *has borne* our sins, He *suffered* in our stead, He *has redeemed* us from the curse, and *"there is therefore NOW no condemnation for sin"* to those who have placed their trust in Him. Sin was judged at Calvary, and those of us who have believed in the finished work of Jesus have already passed from the death which sin demanded into the life which Jesus purchased with His own precious blood.

This does not mean, however, that the born again child of God will not commit sin. God does not *want* His children to sin, but the old, Adamic nature

160

is not taken away when we are born into the family of God. Therefore when we become children of God through the new birth we also become dual personalities—that is, we live in the flesh, but the Holy Spirit lives in our inner man and we possess a new nature. Whether the old or the new nature dominates the life of the believer will depend on which is fed and which is starved. If we feed the flesh, then the flesh will have the victory. If we live in the Spirit and feed on the Word, then we will be victorious, conquering Christians.

The Apostle Paul discusses the warfare between the two natures as related to his own experience after his conversion. (Please study Romans 7:1—25 in connection with this.) The battle between the old and the new natures will continue as long as we live in this world. Only when we depart this life will the old nature be eradicated. Thus, whether he intends to or not, the believer will sin; and sins committed after we are born again must be put away daily by confession, else God will chastise us—for we are sons of God, and "whom the Lord loveth He chasteneth, and scourgeth every son whom He receiveth. If ye endure chastening, God dealeth with you as with sons; for what son is he whom the father chasteneth not? But if ye be without chastisement, whereof all are partakers, then are ye bastards, and not sons" (Heb. 12:6—8).

Furthermore, Paul declares, "If we would judge ourselves, we should not be judged. But when we are judged, we are chastened of the Lord, that we should not be condemned with the world" (I Cor. 11:31, 32). SIN was judged at Calvary; but *sins* in the life of the believer must be confessed and put away, lest God chasten His disobedient child. "If

161

we confess our sins, He is faithful and just to forgive us our sins, and to cleanse us from all unrighteousness" (I John 1:9).

Judgment Number Two:—

"We must all appear before the judgment seat of Christ; that every one may receive the things done in his body, according to that he hath done, whether it be good or bad" (II Cor. 5:10).

This judgment is yet future and it will be for believers only. The *subject* will be believers *in relation to stewardship.* The *time* will be after the Rapture of the Church. The *place* will be the judgment seat of Christ in the air, and the *basis* of this judgment will be "of what sort" our works may be. The *results* will be that some believers will receive a reward while others will suffer loss—loss of reward, not loss of the soul (I Cor. 3:11—15). This will be the crowning day for believers.

Judgment Number Three:—

This judgment is yet future. Its *subjects* will be the Jews, the *time* will be the Great Tribulation period.

The *place* of this judgment will be Jerusalem and surrounding territory. While the Church is at the judgment seat of Christ in the air, the Jews will be judged under the false messiah right here on this earth. Jesus said to the Jews, "I am come in my Father's name, and ye receive me not. If another shall come in his own name, him ye will receive" (John 5:43). Since the Jews are an earthly people, and since all of God's promises to that nation are earthly promises, it follows that their judgment will of necessity be of an earthly character, and that it will take place right here on earth.

The *basis* for this judgment of the Jews is their rejection of the Godhead—Father, Son, and Holy Spirit. In the days of Samuel, Israel rejected God the Father, "and the Lord said unto Samuel, Hearken unto the voice of the people in all that they say unto thee: for *they have not rejected thee, but they have rejected ME, that I should not reign over them*" (I Sam. 8:7). When Jesus came to earth and tabernacled among men, they rejected Him, the only begotten *Son of God*, "and they cried out all at once, saying, *Away with this Man, and release unto us Barabbas*" (Luke 23:18).

In the days of Stephen, the Jews rejected *God the Holy Spirit:* "Ye stiffnecked and uncircumcised in heart and ears, ye do always resist the Holy Ghost: as your fathers did, so do ye" (Acts 7:51). The sermon Stephen preached to them—including the words just quoted—whipped them to frenzy and they rushed upon him and stoned him to death.

Because of their sin in rejecting the Godhead, the Jews have been scattered to the four corners of the earth and have gone through persecution such as no other nation has ever known. When the times of the Gentiles are nearing the end the nation Israel will be gathered back into the Holy Land—unconverted, of course—and caused to pass under the rod (Ezek. 20:33—38). They will be cast into God's melting pot and He will blow the fire of His wrath upon them (Ezek. 22:19—22).

The Jews will pass through an experience spoken of by Jeremiah as "the time of Jacob's trouble" (Jer. 30:7). Daniel 12:1 speaks of that time as "a time of trouble, such as never was since there was a nation." The Antichrist will be the human agent used to bring this terrible judgment upon the Jews. He will be

163

the false messiah, and the awfulness of his rule will be supplemented by the pouring out of the vials of God's wrath, as discussed earlier in this message.

The *result* of the terrible blood bath poured out upon the Jews will be that in their misery and hopelessness they will call on the name of their God (Zech. 12:10). Then Christ will return, they will see Him and will recognize Him (Zech. 13:6). It is then that Israel as a nation will be saved, converted in a day (Isa. 66:8).

This will complete the judgment of the Jews as a nation. They will be ushered into the kingdom, they will receive all of the promises God made to Abraham, and they will occupy that glorious land that flows with milk and honey eternally—the new earth.

Judgment Number Four: —

"When the Son of man shall come in His glory, and all the holy angels with Him, then shall He sit upon the throne of His glory: and before Him shall be gathered all nations: and He shall separate them one from another, as a shepherd divideth his sheep from the goats: and He shall set the sheep on His right hand, but the goats on the left.

"Then shall the King say unto them on His right hand, Come, ye blessed of my Father, inherit the kingdom prepared for you from the foundation of the world. For I was an hungred, and ye gave me meat: I was thirsty, and ye gave me drink: I was a stranger, and ye took me in: Naked, and ye clothed me: I was sick, and ye visited me: I was in prison, and ye came unto me.

"Then shall the righteous answer Him, saying, Lord, when saw we thee an hungred, and fed thee? or thirsty, and gave thee drink? When saw we thee a stranger, and took thee in? or naked, and clothed thee? Or when saw we thee sick, or in prison, and came unto thee? And the King shall answer and say unto them, Verily I say unto you, Inasmuch as ye have done it unto one of the least of these my brethren, ye have done it unto me.

"Then shall He say also unto them on the left hand, Depart from me, ye cursed, into everlasting fire, prepared for the devil and his angels: For I was an hungred, and ye gave me no meat: I was thirsty, and ye gave me no drink: I was a stranger, and ye took me not in: naked, and ye clothed me not: sick, and in prison, and ye visited me not.

"Then shall they also answer Him, saying, Lord, when saw we thee an hungred, or athirst, or a stranger, or naked, or sick, or in prison, and did not minister unto thee? Then shall He answer them, saying, Verily I say unto you, Inasmuch as ye did it not to one of the least of these, ye did it not to me. And these shall go away into everlasting punishment: but the righteous into life eternal" (Matt. 25:31–46).

This judgment is yet future and will be from the throne of His glory here on earth. The *subjects* will be the Gentile nations. The *time* will be when Christ is revealed from heaven with all of His mighty angels, and the *place* will be in the valley of Jehoshaphat. The *basis* of this judgment will be the treatment extended by the Gentile nations toward the Jews during the tribulation period, and the *result* will be that some of the nations will be saved and others will be destroyed.

Many people confuse this judgment with the judgment described in Revelation 20:11–15, but when that passage is carefully compared with the passage just quoted from Matthew's Gospel it will be clearly seen that they are two distinctly separate events. In Matthew there is no resurrection; in Revelation there *is* a resurrection. In Matthew, living nations are judged; in Revelation *the dead* are judged. In Matthew, the judgment takes place here on earth; in Revelation it takes place in the heavens. In Matthew no "books" are mentioned or suggested; in Revelation, "books" are opened, and "another book" is opened. In Matthew, three classes of subjects are named—the sheep, the goats, the brethren; in Revelation, only one class is mentioned—the dead. In Matthew the time is before the Millennium; in Revelation the time is definitely *after* the Millennium.

Also, in comparison of these two passages of Scripture we find that the Greek word translated "nations" in Matthew is found one hundred and fifty-eight times in the New Testament where it is translated "Gentiles" ninety-two times, "nation" or "nations" sixty-one times, and "heathen" five times—but not one time is it applied to the dead or the resurrected!

Since this will be a judgment of *nations,* the Jews will not be in it because God decreed that the Jews "shall not be reckoned among the nations" (Num. 23:9). The *Church* cannot be in this judgment because the saints will be associated with Christ in judging the world (I Cor. 6:2). Therefore the Church will be *with Christ* when He judges the nations. In addition to this, both the Church and the Jews will already have been judged, so it is clear that the judgment of *the nations* cannot be a general judgment where the Church, the Jewish nation, and all mankind will be judged at the same time.

The question then is—*who are the sheep?* Do they not represent the righteous from the beginning of the world to the end of time? and do not *the goats* represent the wicked of all time? Now beloved, if the *sheep* represent the righteous and the *goats* represent the wicked, I ask who on earth can *the brethren* be? If they are the followers of Christ as some people declare them to be, then they should be classed with the sheep. If "the brethren" and "the sheep" are both followers of Christ, why separate them and call them by two different names? The Scriptures teach us that the righteous are saved by faith and the wicked are lost for *lack* of faith—through unbelief; but in this judgment the sheep inherit the kingdom and the goats are commanded to depart because of their treatment of *the brethren.*

Actually, this part of the Scripture is just as clear as John 3:16. The confusion in this matter is caused by trying to make a judgment of *nations* mean a judgment of *individuals.* This is error. The *sheep* represent one class of nations, the *goats* represent another, and *the brethren* represent the Jewish nation, the brethren of the Lord Jesus Christ.

We must also consider the time and place of this judgment. It takes place at the time of the Revelation, when Christ comes to set up His millennial kingdom here on earth, and it takes place in the Valley of Jehoshaphat near the city of Jerusalem, as declared in Joel 3:1, 2:

"For, behold, in those days, and in that time, when I shall bring again the captivity of Judah and Jerusalem, I will also gather all nations, and will bring them down into the Valley of Jehoshaphat, and will plead with them there for my people and for my heritage Israel, whom they have scattered among the nations, and parted my land."

As previously stated, the basis for this judgment will be the treatment of the Jews, Christ's brethren, during the Great Tribulation so minutely described in the book of Revelation. The nations who befriend the Jews during that time will make up the "sheep" nations. Those who refuse to help the brethren of the Lord will make up the "goat" nations. Therefore at the judgment of the nations the King will say to the sheep nations, "Inasmuch as ye have done it unto the least of these my brethren . . . come ye blessed of my Father, inherit the kingdom prepared for you from the foundation of the world!" This is the millennial kingdom which the sheep nations will inherit and possess during the Millennium. Thus the righteous of these nations will enter into the Millennium, but the goat nations will be told, "Depart from me, ye cursed, into everlasting fire, prepared for the devil and his angels"—and the wicked individuals who compose those nations will "go away into everlasting punishment."

Judgment Number Five:—

"And I saw a Great White Throne, and Him that sat on it, from whose face the earth and the heaven fled away; and there was found no place for them. And I saw the dead, small and great, stand before God; and the books were opened: and another book was opened, which is the book of life: and the dead were judged out of those things which were written in the books, according to their works.

"And the sea gave up the dead which were in it; and death and hell delivered up the dead which were in them: and they were judged every man according to their works. And death and hell were cast into the lake of fire. This is the second death. And whosoever was not found written in the book of life was cast into the lake of fire" (Rev. 20:11—15).

This judgment is also in the future. The *subjects* are the wicked dead, the *time* will be during the renovation of the earth by fire, the *place* of the judgment will be the Great White Throne in the heavens.

168

The *basis* will be the works of those who are judged, and the *result* will be that they will be cast into the lake of fire that burns with brimstone forever.

This final judgment will take place at the close of the thousand-year reign of Christ on earth. In II Peter 3:7 we read, "The heavens and the earth, which are now, by the same Word are kept in store, reserved unto fire against the day of judgment and perdition of ungodly men." This definitely pinpoints this judgment as occurring during the time of the renovation of the earth by fire. The Great White Throne judgment will be for the wicked dead. (The righteous dead will rise at the first resurrection when the Rapture occurs.)

Also part of this first resurrection will be the saints of the tribulation period. After the Rapture, the 144,000 Jewish missionaries will preach the Gospel of the kingdom, and a great multitude of every tribe, tongue, and nation will believe and be saved. However, these will be martyred for their faith because they will refuse to receive the mark of the beast in their foreheads and in their hands. These saved ones of the tribulation period will be raised at the end of the Great Tribulation and just before the coming again of the Lord to the earth to set up His millennial kingdom. They are the "gleanings" of the first resurrection (Lev. 23:10; I Cor. 15:23).

The ungodly will not be judged to see whether they are entitled to eternal life, or whether they are entitled to hell. They will be judged to ascertain the degree of their torment. The sad, sad feature of the Great White Throne judgment will be that there will be many kind, morally good people there— but they will not be *saved* people and will be classed among the ungodly because they rejected Christ.

There will be no back-talk, no arguing, because when the books are opened the recording angel will have kept a perfect record and every person's works will be entered in the book. Therefore they will be judged according to their works. Some will be sentenced to a more severe, excruciating punishment than others, but not one will escape the damnation of hell.

Saddest of all, those who are "not so bad" will spend eternity with those who are "very, very bad." Their punishment will include the "second death"—which means that they will lose everything they could have gained if they had accepted life in the Lord Jesus Christ. Death will not be the cessation of existence, but *continual, eternal death,* dying eternally, in the lake of fire.

It is at this time that the fallen angels will be judged. In Jude 6 we read, "The angels which kept not their first estate, but left their own habitation, He hath reserved *in everlasting chains under darkness unto the judgment of the great day.*" When this judgment is over, the devil, the beast, the false prophet, the devil's angels, and all the ungodly will be consigned to the lake of fire and the universe will be completely purged of all evil and unrighteousness. Righteousness will engulf the universe and will reign supreme on the new earth. Never again will anything enter God's new creation that will defile it.

Dear reader, if you are not a child of God I want to call your attention to those who will be your neighbors throughout eternity—unless you accept Christ in this life:

"The beast was taken, and with him the false prophet that wrought miracles before him, with which he deceived them that had received the mark of the beast, and them that worshipped his image. These both were cast alive into a lake of fire burning with brimstone" (Rev. 19:20).

"And the devil that deceived them was cast into the lake of fire and brimstone, where the beast and the false prophet are, and shall be tormented day and night for ever and ever" (Rev. 20:10).

"The fearful, and unbelieving, and the abominable, and murderers, and whoremongers, and sorcerers, and idolaters, and all liars, shall have their part in the lake which burneth with fire and brimstone: which is the second death" (Rev. 21:8).

Surely you do not want to spend eternity next door to the beast, the false prophet, even the devil himself with all of his wicked hosts! I plead with you to give your heart to Jesus this very moment. Believe on the Lord Jesus Christ and He will save you and forgive your sins. That is the only possible way for you to escape the damnation of hell and avoid spending eternity next door to such neighbors as we have listed in the Scriptures just quoted.

The Glories of Christ's Kingdom

"And in the days of these kings shall the God of heaven set up a kingdom, which shall never be destroyed." (The millennial kingdom will merge into the everlasting kingdom—Isa. 9:6,7.) "And the kingdom shall not be left to other people, but it shall break in pieces and consume all these kingdoms, and it shall stand for ever" (Dan. 2:44).

"I saw in the night visions, and, behold, one like the Son of man came with the clouds of heaven, and came to the Ancient of days, and they brought Him near before Him. And there was given Him dominion, and glory, and a kingdom, that all people, nations, and languages, should serve Him: His dominion is

171

an everlasting dominion, which shall not pass away, and His kingdom that which shall not be destroyed" (Dan. 7:13,14).

If we will carefully study these two fundamental passages from Daniel's great prophecy we will clearly see that this promised kingdom will come with the coming of Christ in the Revelation. It will be preceded by a judgment of earth's kingdoms. Nebuchadnezzar beheld this in his prophetic dream of the great image, the meaning of which Daniel interpreted for him in detail.

This is definitely an earthly kingdom, and the saved nations will be gathered into it. Israel, converted at that time, will be back in their own land and the holy city Jerusalem will be the center of activity. The Church—the bride of Christ—will reign with Him over the kingdom.

What will His work be at that time? In the first place, He will speak peace to the "sheep" nations. In Zechariah 9:10 we read, "I will cut off the chariot from Ephraim, and the horse from Jerusalem, and the battle bow shall be cut off: and He shall speak peace unto the heathen: and His dominion shall be from sea even to sea, and from the river even to the ends of the earth." Then will be universal peace. Christ is the Prince of Peace, and in His earthly kingdom men will no longer need weapons of war. They will "beat their swords into plowshares, and their spears into pruninghooks: nation shall not lift up sword against nation, neither shall they learn war any more" (Isa. 2:4).

Then, "with righteousness shall He judge the poor, and reprove with equity for the meek of the earth: and He shall smite the earth with the rod of His mouth, and with the breath of His lips shall He slay the wicked" (Isa. 11:4).

Also in Isaiah 42:1 God declares, "Behold my Servant, whom I uphold; mine Elect, in whom my soul delighteth.   I have put my Spirit upon Him: *He shall bring forth judgment to the Gentiles."*

He will also "set up an ensign for the nations, and shall assemble the outcasts of Israel, and gather together the dispersed of Judah from the four corners of the earth" (Isa. 11:12).

Many nations will be joined to the Lord in that day, and they will be the people of God. He will dwell in the midst of them (Zech. 2:11). "And the Lord shall be King over all the earth: in that day shall there be one Lord, and His name one" (Zech. 14:9).

When Jesus reigns on earth, there will be justice: "Behold, the days come, saith the Lord, that I will raise unto David a righteous Branch, and a King shall reign and prosper, and shall execute *judgment and justice* in the earth" (Jer. 23:5).

The precious words of these Scriptures mean exactly what they say.   We are not to spiritualize the promises given here.   Righteousness, peace, and security will characterize the world-wide, glorious kingdom of the Lord Jesus Christ. His glory, His righteousness, His love and mercy will cover the earth as the waters cover the sea. "In His days shall the righteous flourish; and abundance of peace so long as the moon endureth. He shall have dominion also from sea to sea, and from the river unto the ends of the earth. They that dwell in the wilderness shall bow before Him; and His enemies shall lick the dust. . . . Yea, all kings shall fall down before Him: all nations shall serve Him. . . . He shall deliver the needy when he crieth, the poor also, and him that hath no helper. He shall spare the poor and needy, and shall save the souls of the needy. He shall redeem their soul from deceit and violence: and precious shall their blood be in His sight. And He shall live, and to Him shall be given of the gold of Sheba: prayer also shall be made for Him continually; and daily shall He be praised" (Psalm 72:7—15).

In the glorious day when Jesus reigns on this earth, *every wrong will be righted.* Present-day evils and oppressions will be abolished, together with vice, crime, sickness, poverty, tears, and death. Only Christ has the power to do this. Every Christian should daily pray, "Thy kingdom come"—which means that we would automatically be praying for the day when the Rapture occurs and the risen Lord calls His own up to meet Him in the air, because the catching away of the saints of God will precede the ushering in of the kingdom by at least seven years.

Christ Will Deliver All Creation

"For I reckon that the sufferings of this present time are not worthy to be compared with the glory which shall be revealed in us. For the earnest expectation of the creature waiteth for the manifestation of the sons of God. For the creature was made subject to vanity, not willingly, but by reason of Him who hath subjected the same in hope. Because the creature itself also shall be delivered from the bondage of corruption into the glorious liberty of the children of God. For we know that the whole creation groaneth and travaileth in pain together until now. And not only they, but ourselves also, which have the firstfruits of the Spirit, even we ourselves groan within ourselves, waiting for the adoption, to wit, the redemption of our body" (Rom. 8:18—23).

174

Future: He Will Deliver All Creation

Sin brought a curse upon all creation—the entire universe; and creation still groans and travails in pain waiting for that glorious day when Jesus will *deliver* all creation from the curse of sin. Glorious truth! The condition into which this universe was plunged because of sin will not continue forever. A better day is coming, the day when groaning creation will be delivered from the curse, the day when the lion, the bear, and the ox will eat straw together; the day when little children will play with serpents and not be harmed. (Study the eleventh chapter of Isaiah.)

Such deliverance cannot come through man's ability, nor through the wisdom and goodness of man; nor will it come through man's program to improve upon civilization. Great scientists have attempted to set things in order in this ruined, cursed creation; but man will never be able to bring in the Utopia about which he talks and for which he plans. The things which destroy—heat, drought, storms, earthquakes—these cannot be arrested and brought to an end by the wisdom and power of man.

But *the day will come* when there will be no more storms, no more earthquakes, no more drought or famine. This earth will be one great Garden of Eden. The Lord Jesus Christ, God's only begotten Son, wore the cursed thorns in a crown upon his brow. He who created all things paid for redemption by the shedding of His precious blood on Calvary's cross. And in His own time He will with omnipotent power deliver this groaning, travailing creation from the curse brought about by Adam's sin. In that day, the great vision of Isaiah will be literally fulfilled, as recorded in Isaiah 11:6−9, when "the wolf also shall dwell with the lamb, and the leopard shall lie down with the

175

kid; and the calf and the young lion and the fatling together; and a little child shall lead them. And the cow and the bear shall feed; their young ones shall lie down together: and the lion shall eat straw like the ox. And the sucking child shall play on the hole of the asp, and the weaned child shall put his hand on the cockatrice' den. They shall not hurt nor destroy in all (God's) holy mountain: for the earth shall be full of the knowledge of the Lord, as the waters cover the sea."

Is this a literal kingdom? Yes! Are these literal animals about which Isaiah wrote? Yes! There are absolutely no grounds for spiritualizing this passage from Isaiah. Christ's earthly kingdom, His glorious reign of one thousand years when He will sit on the throne of David in Jerusalem, will be a literal kingdom just as surely as we live on a literal earth today.

All Things Will Be Put Under His Feet

"Blessed be the God and Father of our Lord Jesus Christ, who hath blessed us with all spiritual blessings in heavenly places in Christ: according as He hath chosen us in Him before the foundation of the world, that we should be holy and without blame before Him in love: having predestinated us unto the adoption of children by Jesus Christ to Himself, according to the good pleasure of His will, to the praise of the glory of His grace, wherein He hath made us accepted in the Beloved, in whom we have redemption through His blood, the forgiveness of sins, according to the riches of His grace; wherein He hath abounded toward us in all wisdom and prudence; having made known unto us the mystery of His will, according to His good pleasure which He hath purposed in Himself: that in the dispensation of the fulness of times He might gather together in one all things in Christ, both which are in heaven, and which are on earth; even in Him" (Eph. 1:3—10).

The glorious reign of Christ in all of His kingly glory will be literally fulfilled just as the prophets saw and prophesied its fulfillment. The *"dispensation of the fulness of times"* is the seventh (and last) of the ordered ages which condition human life here on earth, and is identical with the kingdom God promised to David. (Please read II Samuel 7:8—17 and Luke 1:31—33.)

Since the day when Adam sinned, man has carried on a time of oppression and misrule; but all of this will end when the Lord Jesus Christ sets up His kingdom, takes His place on the throne of David, and reigns in righteousness over this earth. The time of Divine compassion and forbearance will end in judgment (Matt. 25:31—46; Acts 17:30,31; Rev. 20:7—15). The time of toil and weariness will end in rest and reward (II Thess. 1:6—8). The time of suffering, heartache, tears, and misery will end in glory (Rom. 8:18). The time of Israel's blindness and severe chastisement will end in conversion and restoration of that nation (Rom. 11:25—27; Ezek. 39:25—29). The times of the Gentiles will come to an end when *the Stone* of Daniel 2:34,35 smites the Gentile kingdoms and the kingdom of God is set up. (Read Revelation 19:15—21.) We should pray daily for God to hasten the glorious hour when all things will come into perfect unity in Christ, that "the dispensation of the fulness of times" will come quickly.

"Then cometh THE END, when He shall have delivered up the kingdom to God, even the Father; when He shall have put down all rule and all authority

and power. For He must reign, till He hath put all enemies under His feet. The last enemy that shall be destroyed is death. For He hath put all things under His feet. But when He saith all things are put under Him, it is manifest that He is excepted, which did put all things under Him. And when all things shall be subdued unto Him, then shall the Son also Himself be subject unto Him that put all things under Him, that God may be all in all" (I Cor. 15:24—28).

King Jesus will put down all rule, authority, and power and will reign until He has put all enemies under His feet—and notice, the last enemy to be destroyed is *death.* He will then deliver up the kingdom to God and will create a new heaven and a new earth—the eternal dwelling place of redeemed and glorified mankind.

A Closing Word to the Unsaved

Dear reader, if you are unsaved and you have read this message, you are interested in your eternal destiny or you would not have read this book from start to finish. So whether you admit it or not, you would like to make heaven your home.

If you have read this book from the first chapter through the last, then you know that God has done everything a loving God can do to keep you out of hell. He loved you so much that He gave His only begotten Son to come into the world and take a body of flesh that He might suffer, bleed, and die on Calvary's cross in order that sinners—including you and me—could be saved from the awful penalty of sin.

God the Son has done all He can do to keep you from spending eternity in hell. He loved you so much that He left the Father's bosom, took upon Himself

178

the form of sinful man, and in that body of humiliation He died for your sins "according to the Scripture." He laid His life down that sinners might *have* life.

In addition to all that God the Father and God the Son have done, the third Person of the Godhead—the Holy Spirit—has done and is doing all that *He* can do to prevent your spending eternity in hell. He came on the Day of Pentecost, He has been here ever since, and it is He who convicts and convinces men of sin. He moved upon holy men of old and spoke through them as God the Father directed, and through His inspiration we have the written Word of God, the message of God which brings salvation.

Jesus said, "He that heareth my Word, and believeth on Him that sent me, hath everlasting life, and shall not come into condemnation; but is passed from death unto life" (John 5:24). Romans 10:17 tells us, "So then faith cometh by hearing, and hearing by the Word of God." The Holy Spirit—He who gave the message of salvation through holy men, bears that message to our hearts as we read or hear the Word. It is the Spirit who convicts us of sin, of righteousness, and of judgment.

The very fact that you have read this book proves that you are convicted of sin, you are convinced that you need a Saviour, and you know there is a judgment day coming when you will have to face a holy God. Whether or not you are ready to meet Him depends on you! The Holy Spirit is wherever *you* are, ready and anxious to "born" you into God's family if you will only receive Jesus into your heart by faith. I urge you, in the light of God's Word, to bow your head right now and ask Him to save you and forgive your sins. Jesus will save you and the Holy Spirit will baptize you into the body of Christ and will take up His abode in your heart.

And dear unsaved friend, I, too, have done the very best I know how to lead you to Jesus. I have prepared this sermon for the primary purpose of helping sinners to be saved. I *want* you to be saved, to know the joy of salvation and the assurance of being a born again child of God. Therefore, if you go on in sin and die and go to hell, whose fault is it? Who is to blame? *Only YOU* can make that final decision, *only YOU* can give your heart to Jesus. You know God loves you, you know Christ died for you, and you know the Holy Spirit is dealing with you this very moment, pleading with you to call on the name of the Lord and be saved! He will write your name in the Lamb's book of life, and you can say with the Apostle Paul, *"I KNOW WHOM I HAVE BELIEVED, and am persuaded that He is able to keep that which I have committed unto Him against that day"* (II Tim. 1:12).

I close this message with salvation Scriptures. Please read them prayerfully. If you will do what these verses tell you to do, you will be saved before you finish reading this book. Believe what God's Word says, pray the prayer the publican prayed— "God, be merciful to me, a sinner"—and you will no longer *be* a sinner. You will be a child of God, saved by His wonderful grace!

"As many as *received* Him, to them gave He power to become the sons of God, even to them that believe on His name: which were born, not of blood, nor of the will of the flesh, nor of the will of man, but of God" (John 1:12, 13).

"For *God so loved the world,* that He gave His only begotten Son, that whosoever *believeth* in Him

180

should not perish, but *have everlasting life.* For God sent not His Son into the world to condemn the world; but that the world *through Him* might be saved. He that *believeth on Him* is not condemned: but he that *believeth not* is condemned already, *because he hath not believed in the name of the only begotten Son of God"* (John 3:16—18).

Jesus promised, "Him that cometh to me I will *in no wise* cast out!" (John 6:37).

"Believe on the Lord Jesus Christ, *and thou shalt be saved,* and thy house" (Acts 16:31).

"If thou shalt confess with thy mouth the Lord Jesus, and shalt *believe in thine heart* that God hath raised Him from the dead, *thou shalt be saved.* For with the heart man believeth unto righteousness; and with the mouth confession is made unto salvation" (Rom. 10:9, 10).

"For *by grace are ye saved through faith;* and that not of yourselves: *it is the gift of God:* not of works, lest any man should boast. For we are His workmanship, created in Christ Jesus unto good works, which God hath before ordained that we should walk in them" (Eph. 2:8—10).

Condescension

I stand amazed in Mary's room
   And hear the message, brought by one,
That God has chosen her to be
   The mother of His only Son.
What word is this? How can it be?
   And yet—submissive to God's plan,
She bore the Burden, all divine—
   For *God Himself* had come to man.

I stand amazed before the cross
   Where One hangs bleeding, wounded sore,
Between two thieves—and 'round Him there
   Men mock and curse, who should adore—
For no mere man is He who hangs
   Upon that cruel Roman tree.
'Tis *God Himself*, enrobed in flesh—
   And He is hanging there for me!

I stand amazed that God Himself
   Should take a robe of flesh, and die,
That I might have eternal life
   And some day dwell with Him on high.
And now He bids me boldly come
   Before His throne, present my plea.
'Tis myst'ry all! 'Tis grace divine,
   That *God Himself* communes with me!

—Georgia Knick Horne